Seven Power
Strategies
for
Building
Customer
Loyalty

Seven Power Strategies for Building Customer Loyalty

Paul R. Timm, Ph.D.

AMACOM
American Management Association
New York • Atlanta • Boston • Chicago • Kansas City • San Francisco • Washington, D.C.
Brussels • Mexico City • Tokyo • Toronto

Special discounts on bulk quantities of AMACOM books are available to corporations, professional associations, and other organizations. For details, contact Special Sales Department, AMACOM, a division of American Management Association, 1601 Broadway, New York, NY 10019. Tel.: 212-903-8316. Fax: 212-903-8083. Web site: www.amanet.org

This publication is designed to provide accurate and authoritative information in regard to the subject matter covered. It is sold with the understanding that the publisher is not engaged in rendering legal, accounting, or other professional service. If legal advice or other expert assistance is required, the services of a competent professional person should be sought.

Library of Congress Cataloging-in-Publication Data

Timm, Paul R.
  Seven power strategies for building customer loyalty / Paul R. Timm.
      p.   cm.
  Includes bibliographical references and index.
  ISBN 0-8144-0569-X
  1. Customer loyalty.   2. Customer services.   3. Customer relations.   I. Title.

  HF5415.5.T515   2001
  658.8'812—dc21

                                                        2001018899

Printing number

10   9   8   7   6   5   4   3   2   1

For
Dr. Sherron Bienvenu, my wife and partner,
and
Jack Wilson of JWA Video, my friend and the man
who got me into the study of customer loyalty

With special thinks to all the really
lousy companies out there that provide
a never-ending source of service horror
stories . . . and the impetus to do better.

Contents

Preface

L oyal customers affect an organization's bottom line more than any ad campaign, marketing program, or PR effort. Turned-off customers produce devastating ripple effects that quickly drag companies into the morass of mediocrity, or worse. The cost of lost customers quickly dissipates any benefits gained from offering quality products, using clever and effective advertising, or implementing cutting-edge marketing taken alone. Nothing enhances organizational success like loyal customers.

The alternative to building customer loyalty is to constantly scramble to replace the inevitably lost ones. It costs five times as much to generate a new customer as it does to keep an existing one. Loyal customers are not only an incredibly valuable resource, they are an intangible form of company capital. The value of the company is dramatically enhanced when customer capital is increased.

Job number-one for any successful organization must be to build customer loyalty. Companies do this by understanding what turns off customers, by holding on to the potentially lost customer, by nurturing "strong relationships," and by exceeding, in positive ways, what customers expect from their experiences with the organization.

This book shows you exactly how to develop customer loyalty. It teaches a powerful strategy that virtually guarantees enhanced customer satisfaction, loyalty, and retention. It teaches seven key strategies that implement A-plus customer service—specific activities that any organization can successfully enact immediately.

This approach does not rely on chance or luck. It provides the tools and direction needed for all members of the organization to play important roles in creating and maintaining customer loyalty. It empowers people. It builds a firm foundation for long-term growth and constant quality improvement.

This book invites you to do more than just read—you are encouraged to interact with the material through self-evaluation activities and numerous worksheets. I think you will find this book fun to read and enjoyable. But most important, I am confident that you will see dramatic results by applying the ideas in the book. When you apply the seven high-impact strategies for building customer loyalty, your customers will ask themselves, Why go anywhere else?

An Important Message to Readers

Throughout this book I make reference to a variety of real organizations. At times I am critical of these organizations and sometimes I offer praise. They serve as both good and bad examples of the ideas I am sharing with you.

Please do not conclude because a company is cited as a poor example that it is necessarily a bad company. All organizations make mistakes and all do many things right. The best of companies can seriously screw up at times. The worst of organizations can come up with brilliant ideas. So, if I give you an example of poor service, don't let that discourage you from seeing for yourself how that company handles your needs. Ultimately, customer service quality is a function of individual customer perceptions.

Seven Power
Strategies
for
Building
Customer
Loyalty

Chapter 1

Getting from Good Intentions to a Strategy

Only mismanagement of customer capital can explain why U.S. companies on average lose half their customers in five years, or why—despite obvious improvements in the quality of manufactured goods, negligible price increases, and un-ending rhetoric about treating customers right—customer satisfaction is actually declining in the United States.
—Thomas A. Stewart, *Intellectual Capital*

The Way It Is . . .

The bank's billboards and TV ads touted the slogan: CURRENTLY GIV-ING 110%. When I asked a teller at my local branch what that meant, she looked at me with a blank stare and said, "I don't know. I just read the sign on my way to work." Does First Security value its customers? Are its employees on board to a coherent service strategy? It doesn't seem like it. A Starbucks coffee shop had two people taking orders and money from the lines of customers waiting. But waiting was the true order of the day. After the customer's order was shouted out, the one young woman charged with actually producing the coffee concoctions was hopelessly bogged down and forced to labor amid widespread grumbling from customers who waited twenty minutes for their cup of java. Does Starbucks have good intentions to serve its customers? Of course. Did they show it? Not today.

A friend bought a television from Best Buy. She got a good price and

1

even sprung for the extended warranty package. After one year the TV developed the annoying habit of shutting down every fifteen minutes. The repair technician came to her home but was unable to fix it. He then took the set to the shop where it lingered for three weeks—never, according to the repair people, exhibiting its quirky behavior. Returned to the customer, the set immediately reverted to narcolepsy.

The customer's calls to Best Buy resulted in endless debate about the fine points of the warranty with a man who claimed to be a customer service supervisor. In short, he wouldn't budge. He frequently put her on hold and came across as totally unsympathetic. The subtext of his message was, "I hope this woman just goes away." Well, good news. She did go away. And she'll take with her anyone who listened to her report of endless wrangling over a TV set. Best Buys spent more time and money stonewalling the customer than it would cost to replace the defective set. For refusing to make good on a $270 television, Best Buy permanently lost this customer. Does Best Buy have good intentions about customer service? I bet they say they do. Did they show it? Not to this customer.

The Disconnection between Service Intentions and Reality

The difference between what companies say about service intentions and what is perceived by customers is strikingly clear. Do companies see this disconnection? And, if so, what do they do about it?

///

Good intentions often get lost in the day-to-day activities and customers notice the disconnection.

///

The first reaction of companies awakening to the need to improve customer loyalty is often to hire consultants or trainers to "motivate their people." They seem to think pep talks can get their people fired up and make them love all their customers. I know this because I have been called upon by numerous companies to perform this miracle. My customer service training gig is pretty entertaining. I get participants involved from the start; we toss out examples of service horror stories with wild abandon. We pinpoint the problems and list ideas for fixing them.

After the sessions, we get new fire in the belly, we're ready to slay those bad service dragons, and we're committed to kicking competitive butt. But then, within a few weeks, things are pretty much back to business as usual. The company thinks it gets points for providing employee training. Managers can display their good intentions—proof positive they are serious about giving good service. But intentions are not enough.

///
It takes more than motivational speeches to get employees involved in building customer loyalty.
///

All companies have good intentions to be customer focused, customer driven, and full of concern for their wonderful customers. Yet many have difficulty translating these good intentions into a meaningful strategy. They really do want to attract and keep happy customers, but they haven't quite figured out the formula for doing so.

Fortunately, help is at hand. This book offers a solid strategy and seven critical tactics for implementing it. With these ideas, any organization can create an ongoing engine for building customer loyalty and creating customer capital. But before we get to that, let's take a closer look at where companies tend to go wrong.

How Companies Go Wrong

Company efforts to build loyalty often fall victim to the problems of ambiguous goals, faulty assumptions, ineffective systems, poor intervention attempts, overreliance on marketing, lukewarm commitment, and lack of measurement. Any of these problems can undercut even the best strategies.

Fuzzy, Ambiguous Goals

For any organizational goal to work, it must be clearly defined and understandable to all who are working toward it. Employees get confused when companies talk about customer service or satisfaction. The clearer goal, that of customer *loyalty*, is sometimes misunderstood. Some think that customer loyalty is just a description of:

//

Every company talks about giving great service . . . about how the customer is always right, the customer is the most important person, yada, yada, yada. So why is it that U.S. companies on average lose half their customers in five years? Why—despite continuous improvements in the quality of manufactured goods, negligible price increases, and unending rhetoric about treating customers right—is customer satisfaction actually declining in the United States?

I think I have found the reason. Companies don't really care; they just pretend to care. If they really cared, they wouldn't do so many dumb things. Here are eight ways you, too, can fake it and create the illusion of caring, without spending a lot of time or effort.

Discerning between Faking It and Making It

1. *Keep service as a separate function or department.* Set up a special department with trained complaint handlers who know all the tricks your customers might try to pull. After all, this is what customer service is really all about. Some of the biggest companies do this. It must work.

Or you could nurture a culture where everyone is equally responsible for serving customers and where such service is recognized as the essence of your business.

2. *Run frequent customer service "programs."* Service improvement programs or special employee incentives must have a starting and ending point. After all, nothing goes on forever, right? Ignore the reality that customer service efforts have no beginning and no end.

Or, you could banish the word *program* and reinforce among employees that service must be an ongoing priority, a core strategy integral to everyone's success.

3. *Use one-shot training.* Hire a high-priced, flashy speaker to get your people jazzed up about customer service. You'll give your employees some new fire in the belly and get them committed to kicking some competitive butt. Important: Do not follow up this training. That will confuse your people. Of course, within a few weeks, things will be pretty much back to business as usual. The company gets points for providing employee training and managers can cite their efforts as proof

positive they are serious about giving good service. This is a great faking technique.

Or you could use training to launch an ongoing strategy. The training could teach people the service behaviors, empower them, reward their involvement, and launch ongoing processes for building customer loyalty.

4. *Equate service with "smilage."* Smiling and being pleasant is really all you need to do to keep customers coming back. If customers have a problem or make an unusual request, be sure to smile when you say "that's not our policy."

Okay, if you have trouble with this idea, maybe you could also give employees the authority to fix things for customers, too.

5. *Rely on marketing tricks.* Instead of focusing on service, keep repeat customers with such things as frequent flier programs or repeat diner discounts. You could imitate the airline mileage programs. Airlines get customers to stick with them even though overall satisfaction among passengers is dropping like a rock. These marketing incentive programs give customers an opportunity to hate their airline more frequently.

Of course, such deals hold customers only until a better offer comes along. Building a real and trusting relationship with customers works far better, but it requires effort and long-term commitment.

6. *Flirt but never get married.* Long-term commitment—now there's a scary idea. Can't we just be friends?

You can, provided you don't mind constantly scrambling to replace the "friends" who went to your competitors. Real customer success depends on ongoing, dare I say, intimate relationships with customers. Locking in customer loyalty requires getting married—getting intimately involved in your customers' needs and wants and creating a symbiotic relationship with them.

7. *Work hard to reduce complaints.* The fewer complaints you hear, the better, right? Oh sure, some idealists argue that you actually want to hear from complaining customers so you can improve your service, but, hey, we all know that's bunk. Teach your employees to make it as difficult as possible for people to complain. Oh, and never mention to your staff that for every one complainer there are likely to be a dozen with the same problem who never bring it up. Those are the customers

you want—the quiet ones. Until, of course, they leave you—which they will.

Complainers are really your best friends and if you make it easy for them to give feedback, and you respond to their feedback, they are actually even more likely to stick with you than if they never have a problem. Anyone can give good service when nothing goes wrong. Fixing problems is the way you show customers you really care.

8. *Avoid measuring your service levels.* Sure, your company accounts for every penny and every tangible resource, but it's normal to throw up your hands in futility when faced with measuring the impact of service efforts. After all, you really can't measure such soft data as customer loyalty.

Tracking that data over time can help you know if you are improving, but you don't really want to know that. It's much easier to fake your sincere interest in customer service.

//

➻ *Customer Satisfaction Alone.* Although satisfaction is a necessary component, a customer may be satisfied today but not necessarily loyal to you in the future.

➻ *A Favorable Response to a Trial Offer or Special Incentive.* We wish it were this simple, but you can't buy loyalty, you have to earn it.

➻ *A Large Market Share.* You may have a large percentage of the customers for a particular product or service for reasons other than customer loyalty to you. Perhaps your competitors are ineffective marketers or your current prices more attractive.

➻ *Repeat Buying Alone.* Some people buy as a result of habit, convenience, or price, but they would be quick to defect to an alternative if a better one is available.

Let's clarify the goal by understanding what we really mean by customer loyalty. Customer loyalty is a composite of five elements:

1. The customer's overall satisfaction. Low or erratic levels of satisfaction disqualify the company for earning customer loyalty.
2. The customer's commitment to make a sustained investment in an ongoing relationship with a company.

3. The customer's intention to be a repeat buyer.
4. The customer's willingness to recommend the company to others.
5. The customer's resistance to switch to a competitor.

When true customer loyalty emerges, relationships grow and ultimately become what Stephen Covey calls "customer synergy." "Synergy," says Covey, "happens when both supplier and customer are changed by the experience, creating something new that neither knew about in the beginning. That experience creates a bonding. Nothing is as powerful as this bonding and, with it, you can leapfrog the competition."[1]

When a company builds customer loyalty and synergy, it is creating wealth in the form of *customer capital*—the organization's intangible wealth that measures ultimate success. Customer capital has been defined as the value of a company's franchise, its ongoing relationship with the people or organizations to which it sells.[2] Companies best build customer capital by fostering customer loyalty. Loyalty is literally a form of wealth.

Customer loyalty → customer relationships →
opportunity for synergy → wealth

Faulty Assumptions about Customers

Sometimes conventional wisdom is off base. Forgive me if I slaughter a few sacred cows, but some overused axioms may be causing you or your people to miss the big picture. Customer loyalty requires that we avoid buying into these oft-quoted but counterproductive ideas.

Faulty Assumption #1: The Customer Is Always Right

The intent of this oft-quoted slogan is probably fine, but by making one party always right, we implicitly set up the other party as wrong. The issue of rightness and wrongness isn't relevant. Using such polar thinking—right versus wrong—precludes getting at the real issue of how we can build mutually useful relationships. If we are attempting to build a better marriage, do we say the husband (or wife) is always right? Of course not. We don't have to choose sides when we look at the goal as being mutual satisfaction and relationship building.

Rightness and wrongness is less important than finding solutions.

If we insist that the customer is always right, then in every dispute the employee must be wrong. What kind of message is that? Who cares who's right or wrong? You're in business to fix problems, not to fix blame; to build relationships, not choose sides.

Faulty Assumption #2: Treat All Customers the Same

Business isn't about democracy or the fairness of equal treatment. To paraphrase George Orwell, writing in *Animal Farm*, all customers are equal but some are more equal than others.

The idea of treating all customers alike stems from a mass-marketing mind-set. But today's successful businesses are less "mass" and more individualized, more "one size fits one." They thrive on recognizing and dealing with individuals, each different. The blind pursuit of sheer numbers of customers—share of the market—runs at cross-purposes with the need to give the one-to-one, personalized service that lies at the heart of loyalty building and customer capital formation.

Treating all customers the same can be counterproductive. Some customers are simply more valuable than others.

A mass-marketing, treat-all-customers-the-same mind-set explains all those credit card applications we find in our mailboxes. Banks are so eager to increase their market share that they overlook the fact that the average bank loses money on three out of five credit card customers— those who use the card only occasionally or pay no interest.

Smart companies treat individual customers differently. Customers who have a greater impact on company success should be afforded additional incentives not offered to less profitable customers. Airline frequent flyer programs, private bankers for high-income individuals, and other organizations that give special incentives to elite customers are not treating everyone equal. They are strengthening relationships with key, profit-generating individuals.

Such special treatment efforts should, of course, recognize long-term potential in customers who may not be currently profitable. As a board member of a credit union associated with a university, I see that many of our current customers (college students) are unprofitable to us—now. Typically these students have little savings and relatively small loan balances. They simply don't generate as much profit as do customers with larger incomes.[3] We still treat them well because we hope for a lifelong, and eventually profitable, relationship.

The best tactic is to treat elite customers special and motivate others to join your elite.

Faulty Assumption #3: It Takes Big Differences to Build Customer Loyalty

The most important underlying premise of any customer service efforts is that *little differences can make all the difference* in the eyes of the customer. People can purchase almost any product or service from several possible sources. The decision to go one place versus another is a zero-sum game. The company either gets the customer or it doesn't.

The customer's choice is almost always dependent on little things, seldom monumental differences between possible providers. An unusually friendly employee, a slightly more convenient location, marginally quicker delivery, better packaging—any of these things can push the customer toward or away from the company. A major theme throughout this book is that little things mean everything and attention to detail counts.

///

Little things can mean everything when it comes to earning customer loyalty.

///

At the core of a customer loyalty strategy is the notion that small, incremental improvements and little surprises given to customers can pay enormous dividends. Once in place and actively managed, the loyalty strategy described in this book will put your company ahead of the pack and pulling away.

Ineffective Systems

A third way companies go wrong in their quest for customer loyalty is in being unaware of the damaging effects of their company systems. The term *systems* often conjures up computers in people's minds, but I am using the term in a broader sense here. Systems refer to any aspect of organizational structure, processes, procedures, policies, or methods used to get the company's products to customers. Systems can range from store location to staffing, from employee training to telephone call handling, from product guarantees to methods of packaging or shipping.

///
Systems are any processes, policies, or methods by which companies get their products or services to their customers.
///

From an organizational structure viewpoint, the worst systems problem arises when the company believes that service is a separate function or department. This tells employees that serving customers is not their main responsibility, it's the responsibility of those guys in the customer service department.

Customer service can never be a separate department. Service is the essence of any business.

If we think the customer service department is a group that handles customer complaints, we will likely train those people to "handle" them quickly and efficiently with a minimum of cost to the company. Too many organizations assume that the fewer complaints you hear, the better.

With that mind-set, the best of all worlds would be the elimination of customer complaints altogether. That would be disastrous for any company. The best companies constantly audit their systems for customer friendliness. Everyone is involved, not just one department or function.

//

No company should have a customer service "department." This function must be at the core of everything the company does.

//

We will talk much more about systems problems that can undermine
loyalty-building efforts throughout this book.

Poor Intervention Attempts

Interventions are the efforts we make to change employee behaviors and
organizational processes to maximize results. Training and development
as well as organizational restructuring are examples of interventions.

Many companies initiate customer service programs or campaigns
aimed at improving some measures. But the description of customer service as a program or campaign implies a start and end point. Customer
service efforts have no beginning and no end. They are ongoing processes
integral to any successful organization.

//

Describing efforts to improve customer loyalty as "programs" implies
that this too shall pass.

//

I recently did a series of training sessions for a medical clinic. The
chief of staff expressed strong concern about patient satisfaction in an
environment of increasing competition. I did workshops for all staff
members and for the doctors. Following the sessions, I contacted the
clinic manager to discuss follow-up. She listened to my reasoning but
never did get around to scheduling additional implementation strategies.
The result: Very little was accomplished. The staff attempted to apply the
ideas taught, but ideas faded and many went back to the old ways.

Too many companies use one-shot training. They hire a flashy
speaker to get employees jazzed up about customer service. They hold
rallies or give great locker-room speeches and hope for the best. Without
follow-up, things quickly get back to normal.

Of course, done correctly, training can launch an ongoing strategy.

It can teach people service behaviors, empower them, reward their involvement, and initiate ongoing processes for building customer loyalty. But company efforts must have legs. The best interventions are ongoing and consistent, not disjointed special events.

Relying on Marketing Tricks or Advertising

Advertising may bring a customer to you, but it has nothing to do with building loyalty. In fact, traditional ads are not even all that good at bringing customers in. Experts looking at the future of advertising see a huge problem as customers try to cut through all the clutter. All the ad messages have become like wallpaper. They are everywhere but no one really notices anymore. Some marketers say "companies may spend the next 1,000 years trying to cut through the clutter they created in the past fifty [years].[4]

One axiom of marketing still holds: Word of mouth is the best possible advertising. Loyal customers tell other people about good companies and products. This process is more powerful than the most elaborate mass-advertising campaign.

//
Word-of-mouth advertising is the most powerful. Loyal customers will do this work for you.
//

Building loyalty with such things as repeat customer programs, discounts, sales, or special deals can hold customers to a point, but only until a better marketing offer comes along. There needs to be something more than marketing tricks to sustain loyalty. A look at the airline mileage programs will show you that, while they get customers to stick with them, overall satisfaction among passengers is dropping like a rock. These marketing incentive programs give customers an opportunity to hate their airline more frequently. Incentives can be helpful but are not a substitute for an ongoing customer loyalty strategy.

Lukewarm Commitment

Companies that behave like those described in the chapter opening seem to have a lukewarm commitment. Many companies do. Producing excellent service and creating customer loyalty are difficult tasks that require a huge commitment. If it were easy, every company would do it.

Lots of companies want to flirt with their customers but never build real relationships or engage in the customer synergy that forges alliances and long-term commitment. Without loyal customers your efforts will necessarily focus on constantly scrambling to replace the customers who went to your competitors. Real customer success requires ongoing, intimate relationships with customers. Locking in customer loyalty requires getting married—getting intimately involved with customer needs and wants and creating synergistic relationships with them.

The commitment must come from the heart of the organization. It must be rooted in corporate values and culture; it must be at the forefront of every employee's mind. This is no small challenge. It requires an unwavering commitment.

//
A commitment to building customer loyalty must come from the heart. Lip service won't cut it.
//

Lack of Measurement

The final common failing of company customer service efforts is failure to measure the results of your efforts. The irony of this is astounding. Companies that account for every penny and every tangible resource throw up their hands in futility when faced with measuring the impact of their service efforts. You must measure the effectiveness of service efforts.

Each chapter in this book suggests ways of assessing effectiveness. Most of the chapters also include self-assessments that help you to look inward at attitudes and behaviors you may be unaware of. Different organizations will choose to measure different things. But, ultimately, the company needs to know to what degree its customers are likely to be loyal. Often such measures must rely on "soft data," but this is no reason to discount their importance.

The simplest way to assess overall customer loyalty is to get answers to three critical questions from customers:

1. How satisfied are you?
2. Do you intend to keep doing business with us?
3. Would you recommend us to a friend?

Some organizations get these answers from every customer. Example: An auto dealership asks all of its customers to fill out a card with these three questions while they wait to ring up their purchases at the service department.

Getting a good, consistent customer sample and tracking that data over time can tell a great deal about loyalty-building efforts. Data—whether soft or hard—can and must be measured.

The Payoff for Implementing Your Loyalty Strategy

The payoff for using the tactics and strategy described in this book will be the enhancement of customer capital. This is accomplished when the organization articulates the value chain, empowers and energizes employees, and commits to continuous quality improvement.

Articulating the Value Chain

The A-plus power strategies you will learn from this book grow out of a value chain model (Figure 1-1) that assesses customers' experiences, responses to those experiences, and the impact of those responses upon the creation of customer capital—that is, organizational wealth. Be certain your people recognize this chain of value derived from creating and maintaining customer loyalty.

The value chain model considers, first, the customer's experience in:

→ Avoiding typical service turnoffs (i.e., value, system, and people problems covered in Chapter 2)
→ Experiencing recovery efforts as problems arise (Chapter 3)

Figure 1-1. The value chain of A-plus service.

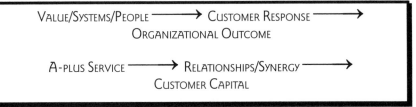

➔ Receiving service that exceeds what was anticipated (Chapters 4–8)

The composite of these customer experiences creates responses. Ideally, this response includes favorable feelings and emotions that lead to relationship building. Finally, the value chain is completed when we evaluate the impact of those customer responses upon the organization and especially on the formation of customer capital. We recognize the value in managing and sustaining the process for continuous improvement (Chapter 9).

Much of the organizational outcome depends on efforts made to create a positive experience for the customer. The customer experience affects bottom-line success. The logic of this approach will become more evident as you read on.

Empowering and Energizing Employees

Building customer loyalty and creating customer capital is a team sport. It requires a coordinated effort and esprit de corps. It requires some risk-taking, some willingness to fail and to learn from failures. Every organizational stakeholder can and should play. The benefits arising from active involvement in ongoing service improvement accrue both to the organization and the individuals who participate.

Participants in strategy implementation will experience a sense of accomplishment and growth. They will see the impact and share in the satisfaction of a job well done. In today's tight labor markets, such fulfillment at work can be an important way to hold on to key players. Energized employees beget healthy, successful organizations.

Committing to Continuous Quality Improvement

The strategies described in this book assume that today's actions can always be improved upon. The bar is constantly being raised, and as companies achieve higher levels of service quality, they strengthen their distinctive competencies.

Continuous quality improvements make it prohibitively expensive for competitors to imitate your level of competence. The more difficult to imitate you become, the stronger your strategic position.

The process described in this book is simple—not necessarily easy, but simple. It calls for the consistent application of seven specific strategies within the framework of participative management and a climate of openness. It requires little extra work for employees and provides an enormous payoff.

The following chapters will teach you the tactics for taking your company far beyond slogans and good intentions as you build customer loyalty.

Application of Worksheets

A good starting point may be to assess where you are now in the minds and hearts of your customers. You need a baseline measure of your current customer loyalty levels. Use the following worksheets as an outline for determining a baseline.

Establish Benchmarks: How Are We Doing?

Each organization will have different effectiveness measures, but one that can be used by anyone is the simple three-question customer loyalty index (CLI). The three key questions this measure asks customers are:

1. Overall, how satisfied were you with [name of company, department, or organization]?

2. How likely are you to do business with [name of company, department, or organization] when future needs arise?

3. How likely would you be to recommend [name of company, department, or organization] to a friend or associate?

Another version of the CLI appears in Figure 1-2 with rating scales and a place for collecting additional customer comments. (As long as you are gathering data, you may as well get some unstructured comments, too.)

Figure 1-2. Customer loyalty index (CLI) form.

Please take a moment to complete this brief feedback card. Your honest reactions and comments as a customer of XYZ Corporation are greatly appreciated. Your input will be used as part of our ongoing effort to provide you with the best possible products and service.

1. Overall, how satisfied are you with XYZ Corporation's products and service? (Circle the number closest to your response.)

Very satisfied		Neither satisfied nor dissatisfied		Very dissatisfied		
7	6	5	4	3	2	1

2. How likely are you to do business with XYZ Corporation again when future needs arise? (Circle the number closest to your response.)

Definitely would		Very likely		Not sure		Not likely		Definitely would not	
7	6	5	4		3	2		1	

3. How likely would you be to recommend XYZ Corporation to a friend or associate? (Circle the number closest to your response.)

Definitely would		Very likely		Not sure		Not likely		Definitely would not	
7	6	5	4		3	2		1	

Please share with us any comments about our products or services:

_____

_____

_____

_____

Thank you for completing this feedback card. Your responses will be used to improve our company's efforts to earn your customer loyalty.

When using Figure 1-2, total the scores for each item and divide this by the number of evaluations filled out. Carry the scores to two decimal points. This information will provide a baseline. This is your starting point. Continue to gather the data over time and compare scores to see if they are improving.

If your company does nothing more sophisticated than gather CLI data on a regular basis, you are doing better than many businesses. Without some such data you will have no idea how to plan or manage your loyalty improvement efforts.

You may, of course, gather additional information from customers, but be careful to avoid overburdening them with long or complicated forms. Also, be careful how you draw your sample of respondents. Either try to get all customers to complete the form or carefully select a random sample. A random sample can be gathered by giving the feedback card to every third or fifth or tenth customer. Do not just give feedback cards to those customers you like or those who may come in more often. Make sampling truly random.

///

When gathering customer data, be careful to either get all customers or a truly random sample. Otherwise your data may be contaminated and unrepresentative.

///

Be Patient about Change

Don't expect CLI scores to change overnight. Changing human behavior takes time and the organizational results may not show up right away. Don't rush the process.

Use measures to set goals, establish priorities, and determine the sequence and timing of your implementation plans. You can't fix everything at once, so look for the kinds of results that can give you the most impact relative to the effort involved. Pick the low-hanging fruit first. Handling the obvious shortcomings can motivate the troops to tackle the more difficult problems later. Use customer feedback of all types to pinpoint turnoffs that need to be addressed.

Managers typically need to budget for improvements. Many

changes, especially those that attack systems or value turnoffs, require the expenditure of money or other resources. Once better methods are developed, establish them as policy—as standing decisions on how the organization is to work.

WORKSHEETS: GETTING FROM GOOD INTENTIONS TO A STRATEGY

✎ CLARIFYING GOALS AND ASSUMPTIONS

Spend some time thinking carefully about your organization's goals and assumptions regarding customers. What do you want to accomplish? Are your goals clear and appropriate? Do you use some mistaken assumptions such as those described in the chapter? Working alone or with a small group, jot down your ideas for changes using the checklist format that follows. List as many ideas as possible without regard for whether they are practical or immediately usable.

Customer Assumptions Your Organization Needs to Change

☐
☐
☐
☐
☐

Review all the ideas you wrote down for possible adoption by your organization. Put a checkmark next to the ideas you want to try.

Next, develop a priority list of the top two or three ideas (you can choose more if necessary), indicating when you will apply each selected idea. Describe tasks necessary to implement your ideas (e.g., the resources needed and assignment of personnel to initiate the task).

Prioritized Improvements	**Implementation Requirements**
1.	Time Frame:
	Tasks:
	Task Responsibility:
2.	Time Frame:
	Tasks:
	Task Responsibility:
3.	Time Frame:
	Tasks:
	Task Responsibility:

✍ REVIEWING SYSTEMS AND INTERVENTION ATTEMPTS

Use this worksheet to brainstorm ideas about your organization's customer loyalty–building systems and intervention attempts as discussed in the chapter. Are you on the right track, or have you made some of the kinds of mistakes described? Working alone or with a small group, jot down your ideas for changes, using the checklist format that follows, without regard for whether they are practical or immediately usable. Then review all ideas for possible adoption by your organization. Put a checkmark next to the ones you want to try.

Ways to Improve Your Organization's Customer Loyalty–Building Systems

☐
☐
☐
☐
☐

Develop a priority list of the top two or three ideas, indicating when you will apply each. Describe tasks or other resources necessary to implement your ideas.

Prioritized Improvements	*Implementation Requirements*
1.	Time Frame:
	Tasks:
	Task Responsibility:
2.	Time Frame:
	Tasks:
	Task Responsibility:
3.	Time Frame:
	Tasks:
	Task Responsibility:

✍ EMPOWERING AND ENERGIZING EMPLOYEES

Use this worksheet to brainstorm ideas about empowering and energizing employees to participate in customer loyalty–building efforts as discussed in the chapter. Working alone or with a small group, jot down your ideas for changes, using the checklist format provided, without regard for whether they are practical or immediately usable. Then review all ideas for possible adoption by your organization. Put a checkmark next to the ones you want to try.

Ways to Empower Employees toward Building Customer Loyalty

☐
☐
☐
☐
☐
☐

Develop a priority list of the top two or three ideas indicating when you will apply each. Describe tasks necessary to implement your ideas.

Prioritized Improvements	*Implementation Requirements*
1.	Time Frame:
	Tasks:
	Task Responsibility:
2.	Time Frame:
	Tasks:
	Task Responsibility:
3.	Time Frame:
	Tasks:
	Task Responsibility:

Notes

1. Stephen Covey, "Customer Synergy," *Customer Service Management* (January–February 2000), p. 66.
2. This definition is attributed to Hubert Saint-Onge in Thomas A. Stewart, *Intellectual Capital: The New Wealth of Organizations* (New York: Doubleday/Currency, 1997), p. 143.
3. Credit unions are not-for-profit and member-owned financial institutions providing financial services for "the little guy." The credit union movement began in the 1930s when common people found that they were generally ignored by banks. Some people argue that the same situation exists today.
4. Jonathan Kaufman, "The Omnipresent Persuaders," *The Wall Street Journal* (January 1, 2000), p. R26.

Chapter 2

Strategy 1: Identify Customer Turnoffs

The single most important thing to remember about any enterprise is that results exist only on the outside. The result of a business is a satisfied customer. Inside an enterprise, there are only costs.

— Peter Drucker, *The New Realities*[1]

The Way It Is . . .

On a recent cross-country trip, my tire blew out on the Ohio Turnpike south of Toledo. It was 6 P.M. on Friday, the temperature hovered in the upper nineties, and traffic was heavy. The right rear tire blew like a bomb and I limped onto the median to dodge the constant flow of rumbling semis. I called the American Automobile Association's hot line on my cell phone. I was greeted by an unsympathetic monotone that mechanically sought my membership card number, expiration date, address, home phone, complete description of my car, my mother's maiden name and middle name of my oldest grandchild, or some such stuff. All the while I am attempting to explain to this voice the imminent danger of being crushed by a big rig roaring by at 80 miles per hour.

"Exactly where are you?" the woman asked. I tried to explain my general location. That wasn't good enough. I'd need to give her an exact mileage marker. So I trekked up the median in ninety-eight-degree heat screaming into the cell phone over the roar of the trucks until I could see a mileage marker. She then told me that a tow truck would be there "in forty-five minutes or less" and that I was to jump out of the car when I saw him coming, to flag him down. This, apparently, was necessary so that he would know *which* white Lexus with a blown-out tire in the median at mileage marker 68 of the Ohio Turnpike was mine.

Fifty minutes later I called for an update. "Any possibility that the truck would actually get here today?" I asked. A different and more sympathetic service rep answered this time, and after going through that membership card number and other information all over again, he told me he would "check to see *if they'd received my call!*" Waiting on hold for four minutes, I was not encouraged. Then, to his credit, he at least apologized ("I'm sorry about the wait; the truck was called to an accident up the road") and promised me the truck would be there in "twenty-five minutes or less." I waited.

This story has a happier ending. The truck driver—Paul it said on his shirt—was a very nice man. He immediately apologized and told me he was fifty miles away when he got the call. He then jumped to work on my tire and I was on the road again. I also had a pleasant surprise: My newly purchased car had a full-size spare tire mounted on a matching wheel. I was anticipating one of those crummy emergency donuts and a trip to the tire store before I could continue my trip. Thank you, Lexus!

Paul was a lifesaver. If I had attempted to change the tire myself, I would have lost it when discovering the special socket for the locking lug nuts. I'm not real mechanical, but Paul knew his stuff and I somehow felt secure in the shadow of his huge towing rig. We chatted pleasantly and he worked efficiently and, although the "forty-five minutes or less" turned out to be an hour and eighteen minutes, I was saved as a Triple-A customer by a tow truck operator named Paul from Toledo, Ohio.

But there were moments when AAA ran a serious risk of losing me, a customer since 1984. Paul's behavior overcame the indifferent telephone behaviors of the AAA employees. And Lexus moved me one step toward customer loyalty by providing a real spare tire.

What Turns Customers Off?

Winning a war requires knowing the enemy. Strategy 1 in our battle for customer loyalty is to know what turns customers off.

My twelve years of research in customer loyalty began with the question, What turns a customer off? In one study (with my colleague, Dr. Kristen B. DeTienne) we gathered open-ended responses to that question. Our content analysis of almost 2,000 collected comments identified three categories of customer turnoffs that disqualify organizations from building customer loyalty: value, systems, and people. The data reveal that the following ten turnoffs accounted for 97 percent of all comments cited by the participants of the study:[2]

Value Turnoffs

+ Poor guarantee, or failure to back up products
+ Quality not as good as expected
+ Price too high for value received

Systems Turnoffs

+ Slow service, or help not available
+ Business place dirty, messy, cluttered
+ Low selection or poor availability of product
+ Inconvenient location, layout, parking, or access

People Turnoffs

+ Lack of courtesy, friendliness, or attention
+ Employees who lack knowledge or are not helpful
+ Employee appearance, mannerisms

///

Customer turnoffs fall clearly into three categories: value, systems, and people.

///

Follow-up interviews and further study seems to confirm that these categories provide a useful framework for identifying root causes of customer dissatisfaction. Let's look at each in more depth.

Value Turnoffs Make Customers Feel Shortchanged

Customers experience a value turnoff when they feel shortchanged on the quality, quantity, reliability, or appropriate "fit" of a product or service.

//

ANOTHER LOOK: CYBER-BLASTING POOR SERVICE

Customers are increasingly using the Internet to voice gripes about companies. One customer tried for eight months to convince Chase Manhattan Bank that he was not responsible for a $690 charge on his credit card. The customer, a former New York University student created a website dedicated to complaints about Chase Manhattan (www. chasebanksucks.com). Another disgruntled airline customer launched a site directed at the unpleasant travel experiences he'd had with United Airlines (www.untied.com). Web visitors are encouraged to post complaints on the site in categories of rudeness, misinformation, incompetence, special needs, and refund problems.

A number of websites have popped up for the purpose of bashing companies and products. A simple Internet search with keywords such as "customer opinion" will point to sites devoted to gripes about corporate giants such as Home Depot, Taco Bell, McDonald's, Wal-Mart, and others. While complainers defend their right to free speech, companies are suffering public relations nightmares over these. Welcome to the world of business today. People are increasingly intolerant of turnoffs and are going out of their way to make their viewpoints known.

//

Being shortchanged is a function of what customers expect. Expectations are influenced by the cost of the goods or services. They don't expect the same thing from low-cost items as they do from more costly ones. But when characteristics of the core product fail to live up to what customers anticipate, they experience value turnoffs.

A quick example: Suppose you have a 79-cent ballpoint pen that quits writing. You may be momentarily annoyed, but you'll throw it away and get another pen. But if the pen that quits cost you $79 instead of 79 cents, you will be much more than momentarily annoyed. Likewise, a $5 fast-food lunch that wasn't so good will be soon forgotten while a $50 dining experience of poor quality will trigger a much more severe reaction.

The responsibility for reducing value turnoffs lies with top leadership in a company. Executive management is ultimately responsible for determining the nature of the products sold. Selling cheap goods may be a perfectly acceptable strategy as long as customers recognize that quality cannot be expected to be as good as a higher-priced alternative. Leaders must determine if they want to be a Mercedes or Hyundai, Nordstrom or Kmart, a full-service bank or a postdated check/quick loan business. Any of these decisions may be fine as long as pricing and perceived value reflect the quality of the products.

Many companies choose a low-cost-provider strategy. Some stores sell only products that cost less than a dollar. Warehouse retailers stack it deep and sell it cheap. This may be a legitimate business strategy and can be profitable. But a company that purports to provide higher-quality products and some semblance of service needs to be certain that customer expectations are being met or exceeded. Companies providing inadequate value are soon discovered and soon out of business.

Systems Turnoffs Inconvenience Customers

Systems turnoffs arise from the way a company delivers its products or services. This entails a wide range of factors—product selection, business location, policies and procedures, customer convenience and comfort efforts, staffing, employee training, and, of course, technology systems as well. As you can imagine, systems problems cover a multitude of sins.

When transactions are unnecessarily complicated, inefficient, or troublesome for us as customers, we experience systems turnoffs. Complaints about long lines, slow service, poor selection, untrained employees, workplace appearance, and poor signage are examples of systems problems.

//
Systems problems arise when customers are inconvenienced.
//

I recently experienced a rather strange systems turnoff with Icelandic Airlines. I was told by an airline representative to confirm my return flight forty-eight hours before flying home. Although I had flown to Iceland six times in the past year, I had never been told to do that before. I dutifully called the airline two days before my flight and met with a phone menu that did not include a selection for confirming flight reservations. I finally selected another choice and, after being on hold for about a minute (while I got to listen to the airline's advertisements), I was connected to a person. The representative sounded a little surprised that I was actually reconfirming my flight! I got the strong impression that this whole call was unnecessary, and I felt mildly embarrassed that I had done what the airline's representative claimed I was required to do.

My research shows that the number-one turnoff for many customers is slow service. In hundreds of training sessions I have conducted across the United States and in Europe, I ask people to identify their "pet peeves" about customer service. In virtually every group, one of the first things cited is slow service or having to wait. We live in a society that values speed and efficiency and resents things that slow us down.

//
A major turnoff for customers is anything that is perceived as wasting their time.
//

Company systems determine the speed of service because they involve staffing, layout of the business, accessibility, and efficiency of delivery, among other factors. The responsibility for implementing and maintaining effective systems lies with a company's management because changes in systems almost always require spending money. A company's decision to add personnel, provide additional training, change locations, implement new delivery methods, or even rearrange the office layout will require management approval.

//
ANOTHER LOOK: PASSWORDS FOR SHOPPERS

A recent study by Jupiter Communications, an e-commerce monitoring firm, looked at a common practice among online retailers that creates annoyance for customers: requiring website visitors to register and provide personal information before they can browse or buy. Jupiter's study concluded that 40 percent of online users are deterred from using sites that require such registration. Microsoft's Expedia Web travel business decided to drop that requirement. Expedia Marketing VP Erik Blachford said, "When you walk into a department store, clerks don't ask for your name and password before letting you shop."[3] A common online procedure has become a systems turnoff for many customers.
//

Employees who lack the knowledge to answer customer questions or organizations that have just one person capable of fulfilling a key function are symptomatic of systems failures. Telephone menus that are unnecessarily complicated (dial 1 for such and such, 2 for so and so) are another common turnoff described by customers. Poor location, lack of delivery options, cluttered workplace, clumsy or repetitious paperwork requirements, lack of parking, or poor selection as a result of inadequate reordering processes are additional examples of systems problems.

People Turnoffs Make Customers Feel Discounted

Customers experience people turnoffs when employees who represent the company project inappropriate behaviors, indifferent attitudes, or a mechanical tone. People turnoffs include rudeness, poor nonverbal behaviors such as lack of eye contact, inappropriate dress and grooming, and any behaviors that convey low caring or consideration for the customer.

///
When employee communication with customers makes the customer feel discounted or unappreciated, you face the possibility of a people turnoff.
///

Responsibility for reducing people turnoffs lies with every employee. Often people are unaware of how their behaviors communicate. Training can help raise awareness, but ultimately the individual staff member decides how he or she will interact with customers.

Because teaching employees specific behaviors is often difficult, hiring people with good attitudes and interpersonal skills is especially important. Some successful employers constantly recruit people they experience in other customer situations. Communication training can help in teaching suggested ways of phrasing comments to customers.

People communicate the way they do because they have learned that behavior. Changes come slowly and only with considerable effort. The best way to change communication behavior is by raising awareness, modeling new behaviors, having people try the new behavior, and reinforcing the improvement. Videotaping can be particularly effective. Companies can benefit from using scripts or scripted phrases and from clearly identifying communication taboos. Let all employees know that certain communications and nonverbal behaviors are unacceptable.

SELF-EVALUATION: WHAT BEHAVIORS SHOULD BE TABOO?

List specific behaviors you feel employees should avoid. Be specific. Use your list as a basis for discussion with other company members (in a staff meeting, for example) and add the ideas of everyone present. Determine how inappropriate behaviors can be replaced. Some examples of taboo behaviors are (but are not limited to):

1. Use of profanity or vulgarity
2. Sitting down when a customer approaches a workstation
3. Inappropriate dress or grooming (your organization must be specific about what is not appropriate, and should get input from employees before implementing a strict dress code)
4. Making derogatory comments about a customer to another employee

---

Here is a brief description of the three turnoffs categorized as applied to my road trip experience:

Value Turnoffs	Systems Turnoffs	People Turnoffs
Had paid my dues for years and never used AAA's road service before; wasn't sure I was getting a good deal.	AAA's policy of saying wait time was "forty-five minutes or less" was initially reassuring, but when the deadline was not met, it was a turnoff. Phone representatives required much information before allowing me to explain my problem.	Phone representative used an unsympathetic tone of voice, displayed no expressions of empathy.

Ultimately, factors that initially turned me off (tone of voice, uncaring attitude, demands for information, inaccurate promises about response time) were mitigated by the good service of a dedicated employee, the truck driver who was personable, friendly, and reassuring. He had expertise and worked efficiently.

And that is largely the point of this discussion. Turnoffs happen. By applying Strategy 1, we can recognize and categorize them, assign responsibility, and attack them. The other strategies presented in this book show ways to mitigate the turnoffs and hopefully eradicate them.

Reducing Customer Turnoffs Is the Best Advertising

No company can succeed if it lets turnoffs aggravate its customers to the point that they quit doing business with it. A typical company will lose 10 percent to 30 percent of its customers each year because it turned them off. This touches off a treadmill-like scramble to replace the lost with new customers—an effort- and cost-intensive process. A far more efficient process is to keep and build upon the current customer base.

Customer loyalty is like an election held every day, and people vote with their feet. If dissatisfied, they walk (sometimes run) to a competitor. When customers cannot realistically switch to another company (in the case of a public utility or government agency, for example), they use their feet for something else: They kick back with anger or animosity directed toward the organization and its employees. The psychological toll of this kicking can be high employee turnover and additional costs to retrain or replace burned-out workers.

///

The ultimate cost of customer turnoffs is both loss of the consumers and potential loss of the employees who get sick of hearing all the complaints.

///

Some people think that advertising is a good way to induce people to buy. In fact, U.S. business spends about $11.5 billion a year on advertising. Yet surveys show that only 25 percent of those polled said that a television ad would induce them to buy. Likewise, only 15 percent and

13 percent respectively said that newspaper or magazine ads caused them to buy. In short, traditional advertising has little confidence among consumers. Ads can create awareness, of course, but they often fail to make people buy.

Advice or the recommendation from a friend or relative, however, scored 63 percent as a determinant of people's buying a new product.[4] This confirms what people have long known: Word of mouth is still the best way to attract customers.

///

Mass advertising may get some people to try a business, but positive word of mouth from happy customers is far more effective at keeping customers.

///

To sustain repeat business, generate positive word of mouth by reducing the turnoffs and exceeding customer expectations. People talk to others about a service experience when it is exceptional, out of the ordinary. Bad news travels faster and further than good news. A company can have the best products available, but if it fails to minimize customer turnoffs and provide a positive customer experience, few people will notice the difference between that company and its competition. We will talk a lot more about exceeding expectations in later chapters.

The Cost of the Lost Customer

Some employees don't understand the real cost of a lost customer. When an unhappy customer decides to stop doing business with a company, the costs are almost always more than people realize. To get a clearer view of the cost impact of a lost customer, let's use a business we are all familiar with: a grocery supermarket. Here's a story of Mrs. Williams.[5]

Harriett Williams, a sixtysomething single woman, has been shopping at Happy Jack's Super Market for many years. The store is close to home and its products are competitively priced. Last week, Mrs. Williams approached the produce manager and said, "Sonny, can I get a half head of lettuce." He looked at her like she was crazy and curtly said, "Sorry, lady. We just sell the whole head." She was a bit embarrassed but accepted his refusal.

Later she had several other small disappointments (she wanted a quart of skim milk and the store only had half-gallons), and when she checked out her groceries she was largely ignored by the clerk, who was carrying on a conversation with another employee. The clerk made matters worse by abruptly demanding "two forms of ID" with Harriett's check (What do they think I am, a common criminal? thought Mrs. Williams) and by failing to say thank you.

Mrs. Williams walked out of the store that day and decided that she was no longer going to do business there. Although she had been a Happy Jack's customer for many years, she realized that Happy Jack's employees couldn't care less if she shopped there. She had been spending about fifty hard-earned dollars there every week, but that was going to change. She felt that, to the store employees, she was just another cash cow to be milked without so much as a sincere thank you. Nobody cared whether she was a satisfied customer.

But today is different—no more "nice" Mrs. Williams! Today she decided to buy her groceries elsewhere. Maybe—just maybe—there is a store where they'll appreciate her business.

Do Lost Customers Impact Employees?

What do the employees think about Mrs. Williams's decision to shop elsewhere? They're not worried. Life is like that. You win some; you lose some. Happy Jack's is a big chain and doesn't really need Mrs. Williams. Besides, she can be a bit cranky at times and her special requests are stupid. (Who ever heard of buying a half head of lettuce?) They'll survive without her $50 a week. Too bad she's unhappy, but a big company can't twist itself into contortions just to save one little old lady from going down the street to the competition. Sure, we believe in treating customers well, but we're businesspeople. Look at the bottom line. After all, it can hardly be considered a major financial disaster to lose one little customer like Mrs. Williams. Or can it?

The employees at Happy Jack's need to understand some economic facts of life. Successful businesses look long term. They look at the ripple effects of their service, not just at the immediate profit from an individual purchase.

The shortsighted employee sees Mrs. Williams as a small customer dealing with a big company. Let's change that view: Look at the situation from another, broader perspective.

The loss of Mrs. Williams is not, of course, a $50 loss. It's much, much more. She was a $50-a-week buyer. That's $2,600 a year or $26,000 over a decade. Perhaps she would shop at Happy Jack's for a lifetime, but we'll use the more conservative ten-year figure for illustration. But that's only the tip of the iceberg lettuce.

What Are the Ripple Effects?

And then there are the ripple effects that make it much worse. Studies show that an upset customer tells on average between ten and twenty other people about an unhappy experience. Some people will tell many more, but let's stay conservative and assume that Mrs. Williams told eleven of her friends. The same studies say that these eleven people may tell an average of five others each. This could be getting serious!

How many people are likely to hear the bad news about Happy Jack's? Look at the math:

Mrs. Williams	1 person
tells eleven others	+ 11 people
who tell five each	+ 55 people
Total who heard =	67 people

Are all 67 of these people going to rebel against Happy Jack's? Probably not. Let's assume that of these 67 customers or potential customers, only one-quarter of them decide not to shop at Happy Jack's. Twenty-five percent of 67 (rounded) is 17.

Assuming that these 17 people would also be $50-a-week shoppers, Happy Jack's stands to lose $44,200 a year, or $442,000 in a decade, because Mrs. Williams was upset when she left the store. Somehow giving her that half head of lettuce doesn't sound so stupid.

Although these numbers are starting to get alarming, they are still conservative. In many parts of the country, a typical supermarket customer actually spends about $100 a week, so losing a different customer could quickly double these figures.

How Much Does It Cost to Replace Customers?

Customer service research says that it costs about five times as much to attract a new customer (mostly through costly advertising and promotion) than it does to keep an existing one (where costs may include giving refunds, offering samples, replacing merchandise, or giving a half head of lettuce). One report put these figures at about $19 to keep a customer happy versus $118 to get a new buyer into the store.

Again, some quick math shows the real cost of losing Mrs. Williams as a customer:

Cost of keeping Mrs. Williams happy $ 19.00
Cost of attracting 17 new customers $2,006.00

Now let's make our economic facts of life even more meaningful to each employee.

How Can Lost Customers Mean a Lost Job?

Calculating the amount of sales needed to pay employee salaries is a fairly simple process. Assuming that a company pays 50 percent in taxes and earns a profit of 5 percent after taxes (typical figures), Figure 2-1 shows how much product must be sold to pay each employee (in three different salary levels) and maintain current profit levels.

These figures will vary, of course, depending on taxes and benefits costs. But the impact on an employee's job can be clearly shown.

If a $10,000-a-year part-time clerk irritates as few as three or four

Figure 2-1. Sales needed to sustain a job.

Salary	Benefits	After-Tax Cost	Sales Needed
$25,000	$11,500	$18,250	$365,000
$15,000	$ 6,900	$10,950	$219,000
$10,000	$ 4,600	$ 7,300	$146,000

customers in a year, the ripple effects can quickly exceed the amount of sales needed to maintain that job. Unfortunately, many organizations have employees who irritate three or four customers a day! Ouch.

SELF-EVALUATION: APPLYING THE MRS. WILLIAMS EXAMPLE TO YOUR COMPANY

Take a few moments and go back to the Mrs. Williams example, but instead use your own organization. Suppose that you lose one customer and the other statistics hold true. Take a few moments to estimate the numbers as they apply to your organization. Consider how often customers typically buy and how much they spend. If you work for a nonprofit or government agency where dollar sales are not a relevant measure, calculate the number of people who may be aggravated or upset with you and your organization. Think in terms of the psychological price that must be paid as you deal with frustrated, angry, upset patrons on a day-to-day basis.

Calculating the Cost of Your Lost Customer

A. Average or typical dollar amount spent (per week or month as appropriate): $_____ per (customer)

B. Annual dollar amount (weekly figure % 52 or monthly % 12) $_____

C. Decade dollar amount (B % 10): $_____

D. Ripple effect costs (B % 17, or the number of people who may follow an unhappy customer out the door): $_____

    Total Annual Revenue Lost (A + B + C + D) $_____

Then

E. Add in the customer replacement cost of 17 customers % $118 (which represents a typical figure):   + $2,006.00

F. Subtract the cost of keeping your present customer happy ($19 is a typical figure):   − $ 19.00

G. Calculate "replacement" costs (E − F): = $1,987.00

Finally,

Total the revenue lost figures (B or C + F)
to arrive at a rough cost of your lost: $\underline{}

Note that these calculations are designed only to get you thinking about the ripple effects of unhappy customers. Their mathematical precision is not guaranteed, nor is it that important. The point is, lost customers cost you, both in reduced revenue and psychological stress.

The first tactic for implementing the A-plus strategy is to understand customer turnoffs and work to minimize them. This is a team effort. Employees need to be aware of the kinds of things that turn customers off, as well as the economic impact of lost customers. Use the worksheet provided here to identify customer turnoffs that could be inflicting damage on your organization. The value-systems-people distinctions described in this chapter can help in identifying and assigning responsibility for dealing with customer turnoffs.

WORKSHEETS:
CHECKING ATTITUDES ABOUT
CUSTOMER TURNOFFS

✎ YOUR EMPLOYEES' ATTITUDES

Circle Y, N, or S to indicate yes, no, or sometimes for each of the following statements. For each N or S answer, indicate specific training or information your people could use to better identify the turnoff and deal with it.

The people in my organization:

1. Clearly recognize the high costs of the lost customer and the long-term value of keeping customers.   Y   N   S

2. Can identify the sources of customer turnoffs and are sensitive to the need to minimize them.   Y   N   S

3. Look at our service through the eyes of our customers by using a variety of tools (e.g., conducting shopper surveys, evaluating our phone techniques, and checking our systems and policies).   Y   N   S

4. Know how to report examples of customer inconvenience to appropriate managers.   Y   N   S

5. Understand that companies sometimes must take a short-term loss or incur a cost to keep long-term customer loyalty.   Y   N   S

6. Regularly track what kinds of concerns our customer have.
Y   N   S

7. Frequently ask customers to comment on our service and offer suggestions for improvement.   Y   N   S

8. Try hard to make our company a fun place to work.   Y   N   S

9. Are communicated with openly and frequently to be sure they know all about our products, policy changes, incentive programs, and future plans for the company.   Y   N   S

10. Are committed to doing whatever is necessary to build and maintain long-term relationships with our customers.   Y   N   S

Score 3 points for each yes, 2 points for each "sometimes," and 0 for each no, then add the points for your total.

Total score: _____

Next, pick two or three "no" or "sometimes" responses and set priority goals for improvement.

Priorities for Improvement	*Training or Other Solution Required*
1. _____	_____
2. _____	_____
3. _____	_____

🖎 THE USUAL SUSPECTS

List the key V-S-P (value-systems-people) turnoffs you suspect your customers now experience. Use this, and if needed, a separate page for this exercise.

Notes

1. Peter Drucker, *The New Realities* (New York: HarperCollins, 1989), p. 6.
2. Paul R. Timm and Kristen B. DeTienne, "How Well Do Businesses Predict Customer Turnoffs? A Discrepancy Analysis," *Journal of Marketing Management*, Vol. 5, No. 2, Fall/Winter 1995, pp. 12–23.
3. Frank Barnako, "Expedia Drops Registration," *InfoBeat*, an online newsletter sponsored by CBS MarketWatch (January 4, 2000).
4. K. Goldman, "Study Finds Ads Induce Few People to Buy," *The Wall Street Journal*, October 17, 1995, p. B6.
5. Bernice Johnson, president of Milestone Unlimited, Inc., Portland, Oregon, commenting in a letter to the editor of *FAST COMPANY* (April–May, 1998), p. 32.

Chapter 3

Strategy 2: Recover Dissatisfied Customers

Those who enter to buy, support me. Those who come to
flatter, please me. Those who complain, teach me how I may
please others so that more will come. Those only hurt me
who are displeased but do not complain. They refuse me permission to correct my errors and thus improve my service.
—Retailing pioneer Marshall Field

The Way It Is . . .

Sally went to her local supermarket. It was a busy afternoon, she was
tired from working all day, and the store was busy. At the checkout,
the clerk let an apple slip out of the plastic bag and drop to the floor. The
clerk started to put it back in the bag and Sally said, "Hold it. I don't
want an apple that's been on the floor." The clerk said, "You can go back
to the produce department and get another one." Sally didn't want to
delay the line anymore and was too tired to go do that.

A young man who was bagging groceries at the next counter over-
heard this conversation and offered to get her another apple. As he jogged
off to the back of the store, Sally apologized to the people behind her in
line. She was about to tell the clerk to just skip it, when the young man
came back, panting slightly, and handed her a beautiful apple, saying,
"Sorry for the delay." He then brought his other hand from behind his
back, adding, "And here's another one for your inconvenience."

Peter's favorite eatery a few blocks from his downtown office had the best southern home cooking, complete with fresh baked biscuits. The owner of the restaurant personally greeted each customer and the food was delicious. One day as Peter paid for his meal the owner asked if everything was okay. Peter half-jokingly mentioned that the biscuits weren't as warm as usual. The owner immediately handed his money back. Peter tried to pay him, saying the meal was fine, just not quite as great as it usually is. The owner would hear nothing of this and refused to accept payment. Peter continues to be a regular customer.

A tiny, almost insignificant gesture reconfirmed in Sally's mind that her grocery store is the place she wants to shop. A restaurant owner's demonstration that he wants only 100 percent satisfied customers secured Peter as a loyal customer.

Hearing and addressing customer complaints is a crucial strategy in building customer loyalty. And as with so many things today, e-commerce has turbocharged this process. Several new companies are building websites for collecting customer feedback (especially complaints). Customers can go to sites such as eComplaints.com to describe their experiences. The goal of eComplaints.com and some budding competitors is to encourage consumers to vent their wrath. These companies then collate, cross-reference, and sell these complaints as marketing research. The intended buyers: the same companies enduring public web whippings.[1] The degree to which these web companies succeed will depend on how serious companies are about getting customer feedback. The best companies will jump at this opportunity to hear from their customers, especially the complaining ones.

Service Glitches Are Opportunities

Any company can give adequate customer service when everything goes well. A smooth transaction is easy. But when glitches occur—when customers have problems or are even a little bit disappointed—the great companies quickly distinguish themselves.

///
Successful companies view recovery as an opportunity.
///

Service recovery is also best accomplished when seen as an opportunity rather than a painful chore. Granted, most of us would prefer not to hear about customers' dissatisfaction. That's human nature. But given that dissatisfaction is inevitable, why not see recovery as an opportunity and challenge? Customer complaints are opportunities to cement relationships. The vast majority of such relationships are worth saving, although occasionally—I stress *occasionally*—we need to let go of the chronic complainer, as we'll discuss later in this chapter.

Customers who complain and have their problems addressed are more likely to become loyal—even more likely than customers who never have problems.

The task at hand, then, is to help your employees see that a complaining customer can be your company's best friend. Then your next job is to:

→ Make it easy for your customers to complain.
→ Act upon such complaints quickly and efficiently.

Make It Easy for Customers to Complain

Dissatisfaction happens. What we choose to do about it can make all the difference in creating customer loyalty. In order to do something about customer dissatisfaction, we need to know when it is happening—we need to get the silently dissatisfied customer to speak up.

Create Open Communication

Open communication occurs best when people feel that their opinion is valued and that they will be rewarded (or at least not punished) for expressing it.

It is rarely pleasant to express a complaint, although some people are more comfortable with it than others. Most people want to maintain cordial relationships and fear that expressions of dissatisfaction will upset others. Our job, then, is to let people know that we are sincerely open to their comments, whether negative or positive. This requires more than just lip service.

//

Successful handling of customer complaints can solidify customer loyalty and be a gold mine of repeat business. Surveys by the U.S. Office of Consumer Affairs reveal some interesting facts:

1. One customer in four is dissatisfied with some aspect of a typical transaction.
2. Only 5 percent of dissatisfied customers complain to the company. The vast "silent majority" would rather switch than fight. They take their business elsewhere.
3. A dissatisfied customer, on average, will tell twelve other people about a company that provided poor service.

Think about this: If 25 percent of customers are unhappy with a company's service but only 5 percent of that 25 percent bother to complain (yet each unhappy customer tells a dozen others), the impact can be devastating. For simplicity, let's say a company serves 100 customers per day. Twenty-five of them are dissatisfied, but the company hears only one or two complaints. That may sound good to management until it realizes that the twenty-three quiet ones are likely to tell 274 other people about the unsatisfactory service!

On average, only 5 percent of unhappy customers bother to complain.

Companies that recover the one or two complaining customers may be saving a dozen others. Enlightened companies can also boost the number of complainers they hear from. Handling complaints from two or three dissatisfied people can save thirty or forty possibly defections. And it can teach the company what it needs to know to improve.

Further good news for companies that learn to effectively solicit and handle complaints is that such companies can charge an average of 8 percent to 15 percent more than their competitors, even in businesses where competition is keen. Example: Maytag, the quality home appliance maker with the "lonely repairman" campaign, supports a premium-priced product in a highly price-sensitive market.

The best news of all is that customers who have their complaints handled well are very likely to do business with the company again. While only 9 percent to 37 percent of dissatisfied customers who don't complain report a willingness to do business with the same company again, fully 50 percent to 80 percent of those whose complaints are fully resolved will consider doing repeat business—even if their complaints were not resolved in their favor.[2] Other findings put this number even higher.

//

Seek Input at the Point of Contact

Most companies have some sort of formal feedback system, ostensibly to gather data that could make service better. These systems, if well designed, can show historical trends and even measure customer loyalty rates. Yet the information they provide is often too little, too late, and too broad-brush. The time to gain specific, useful insights from an unhappy customer is at the point of contact and the time of the problem. For holding on to potentially lost customers, less formal approaches are better. Creating a climate in which people give real-time, on-the-spot feedback may be more important than a printed customer feedback card, telephone follow-up, or focus group.

Reinforce, Don't Challenge, the Customer

You create such a climate by reinforcing customer behaviors, not challenging them. The natural tendency is to react to complaints with some defensiveness. Instead, we should react with encouragement. An auto dealership service manager I know does a good job in this regard. I called to tell him of a funny noise coming from my car after it had just been serviced. Instead of asking me a bunch of questions about the kind of noise, or, worse yet, implying in some way that the noise may be my fault, he immediately said, "That's not good. We better get that fixed for you." I didn't have to explain, justify, or diagnose (although he later—and tactfully—asked for some additional details about the nature of the noise). I told him of my complaint and he immediately projected an attitude of "let's get this fixed for you."

//
When customers complain, avoid challenging them. Instead take an immediate let's-fix-it attitude.
//

Such an attitude will reduce the likelihood of shutting down a customer before he or she has an opportunity to complain. It opens up the possibility that you will not only recover this customer, but avoid bad press with a dozen or so other people.

Be Sensitive to First Reactions

The first comments out of your mouth when a customer begins to complain will largely determine the quality and quantity of feedback you will get. Like my auto service guy, make it positive and helpful.

Avoid acting defensive or making unnecessary demands for details. Accept the fact that the complaint is legitimate because it is real to the customer. Don't justify or even explain your side until you hear the whole story. Maintain eye contact and use nonverbal behaviors that show your interest in hearing it all. Be careful of facial expression (e.g., a smirk or look of boredom) that may discount the customer. If your contact is by phone, avoid dead air or prolonged silences that may convey skepticism or lack of interest.

///

Be responsive and immediately express willingness to help when a customer complains.

///

Avoid any comments that would be construed as challenging the customer. If you suspect that the problem may be caused by customer misuse of the product, wait until the whole complaint is expressed and then ask some tactful questions about how the product was used. The issue is not whether the customer or the company is "right." The productive attitude is one of cooperation and problem solving that wins a loyal customer.

SELF-EVALUATION: WHAT ARE YOUR FEELINGS ABOUT DEALING WITH DIFFICULT CUSTOMERS?

I've listed here a series of words that may describe the ways you feel about dealing with upset customers. Select the five words that most describe your general feelings.

afraid	angry	anxious	apathetic	bored
calm	cautious	comfortable	confident	confused
contented	distraught	eager	ecstatic	elated
excited	foolish	frustrated	glad	hesitant
humiliated	joyful	nervous	proud	relieved
sad	silly	uneasy	uncomfortable	wishful

My top five words:

1. _____   4. _____

2. _____   5. _____

3. _____

The words you identified above may convey something about your attitudes. They can become self-talk, which is often self-fulfilling. If you consistently label your reaction as uncomfortable or anxious or bored, you
may project these feelings to the customer. If complaints trigger feelings
such as confidence or eagerness to help, you will also convey these reactions to customers.

When you have finished this chapter, review the words you selected
again to see if you have some better ideas on how to deal with these
emotions. Discuss your results with a small group, asking for feedback on
how to deal with the feelings you have.

How You Can Best Act upon Complaints

As soon as you detect or even suspect that a customer is less than fully
satisfied, take action. Early recovery is far easier than letting a bad situation fester and then trying to fix it. Act on complaints quickly, tactfully,
and efficiently using a three-step process of conveying empathy, resolving
the problem, and offering something more to exceed what the customer
anticipates.

Feel the Customer's Pain

The first step in developing recovery skills is to recognize that upset customers are likely to be disappointed, angry, frustrated, or even in pain,

and they blame you to some extent. Typically they want you to do some or all of the following:

- ✦ Treat them with respect and empathy.
- ✦ Listen to their concerns, understand their problem, and take them seriously.
- ✦ Compensate them or provide restitution for the unsatisfactory product or service.
- ✦ Share their sense of urgency; get their problem handled quickly.
- ✦ Avoid further inconvenience.
- ✦ Punish someone for the problem (sometimes).
- ✦ Assure them the problem will not happen again.

Some employees have trouble knowing how to express concern to an upset customer. One model for communicating in such situations is called the "feel, felt, found" approach.

The "feel, felt, found" approach expresses empathy. Seminar leader and author Rebecca Morgan teaches people how to question people and express ideas so that upset customers won't become more upset.[3] The 3 F's are a skeleton on which to hang the rest of your response to a customer. This technique acknowledges the customer's feelings and offers an explanation in a way she can listen to. Often you can use this exact wording:

- ✦ "I understand how you could *feel* that way."
- ✦ "Others have *felt* that way, too."
- ✦ "Our other customers then *found,* after an explanation, that this policy actually protects them, so it made sense."

The first two statements can be used verbatim. The third is an opportunity to explain what can or cannot be done to help solve the problem.

Try using the 3 F's approach, but be careful how you word your statements. Don't say, "I *know* how you feel" (no one can really know exactly how another person feels), but do say, "I can understand how (or why) you'd feel that way."

Do All You Can to Resolve the Problem

When attempting to recover an unhappy customer, the icing on the cake is the "something extra" you give by way of making up for the problem.

Suppose you buy a new pair of shoes and the heel falls off. You call the shoe store and the owner says to bring them back and he'll replace them. You take time off from work, drive downtown to the store, battle for a parking space, and spend about an hour doing it all. He cheerfully gives you a new pair of shoes. Are you satisfied now?

Probably not. Why? Because he really hasn't repaid you for the inconvenience. Sure, the manager stood behind the product and perhaps even did so in a pleasant manner, but you still came out on the short end.

///
Anytime a customer must complain, it is an inconvenience that should be made up for if possible.
///

Go Beyond by Offering "Symbolic Atonement"

What kinds of things can we do to make up for the problem? Here are a few possible ideas that in the eyes of a customer could be seen as going the extra mile:

→ *Offer to pick up or deliver goods to be replaced or repaired.* Auto dealerships win loyalty by offering to pick up the customer's car rather than have the customer bring it in when a recall notice requires something to be fixed

→ *Give a gift of merchandise to repay for inconvenience.* The gift may be small, but the thought will be appreciated. Customer service expert Ron Zemke calls this "symbolic atonement." Examples include a free dessert for the restaurant customer who endures slow service, or extra copies of a print job to offset a minor delay. It's the thought that counts.

→ *Reimburse for costs of returning merchandise.* That might mean picking up parking fees, for example, if the customer has to actually return to your location. Mail-order retailers pay all return postage fees to reduce customer annoyance and inconvenience.

→ *Acknowledge the customer's inconvenience.* Even thank the customer for giving you the opportunity to try to make the problem right. A sincere apology can go a long way. Make the wording of the apology sincere and personal. Say, "I'm sorry you had to wait," rather than, "The company regrets the delay." Empathy can be expressed with statements such as, "I know how aggravating it can be to . . ." or "I hate when that happens, and I'm sorry you had to go through. . . ."

➔ *Follow up to see that the problem was handled.* Don't assume the customer's difficulty has been fixed unless you handled it yourself and have checked with the customer to see that the fix held up.

Look for creative ways to make up for, or at least offset, some of the inconvenience.

You may not have the authority to take all of these actions (although many of them cost practically nothing), but you can go to bat for the customer with your boss. Just being the customer's advocate can help reduce much of the problem. If all goes well, you should feel a genuine sense of satisfaction after handling an unhappy or irate customer.

Keep Emotion out of Recovery

Often you can creatively recover an unhappy customer. But this is not a perfect world and people are not always rational. Sometimes they get to you and you get upset. Work to avoid letting anger or frustration reflect back on that customer or other customers. Although it may be difficult, to succeed, remember these key points:

➔ *Don't beat yourself up.* If you try your best to satisfy the customer, you have done all that you can do.

➔ *Don't take it personally.* Upset people often say things they don't really mean. They are blowing off steam, venting frustration. If the problem was really your fault, resolve to learn from the experience and do better next time. If you had no control over the situation, do what you can, but don't bat your head against the wall.

➔ *Don't rehash the experience with your coworkers or in your own mind.* What's done is done. Recounting the experience with others probably won't make their day any better, and rehashing it to yourself will just make you angry. You may, however, want to ask other people how they would have handled the situation.

//

Use every customer contact experience as an opportunity to improve
your service professionalism. Even the most unpleasant encounter can
teach useful lessons.

//

Look Back and Learn

When the customer situation has cooled, you may want to review how
you handled the customer with an eye toward improving your skills.
Think back on the situation and ask questions such as these:

+ What triggered the customer's complaint? Was it primarily a
  value-, systems-, or people-generated problem?
+ What would it take to fix such a problem? Is it possible to avoid
  it altogether?
+ How did the customer see the problem? Who was to blame, what
  irritated the customer most, why was the customer angry or frus-
  trated?
+ How did you see the problem? Was the customer partially to
  blame?
+ What did you say to the customer that helped the situation?
+ What did you say that seemed to aggravate the situation?
+ How did you show your concern to the customer?
+ What would you do differently if a similar complaint arose?

How Should You Handle the Occasional
Customer from Hell?

"Stubbornness is the energy of fools," says the German proverb. Sometimes we need to draw the line between upset customers with legitimate
problems and chronic complainers who consume our time with unreasonable demands—the dreaded "customer from hell."

//

Chronic complainers, although rare, require different treatment.

//

Be Sure the Person Really Is a Chronic Complainer

Step one in dealing with such people is to be sure you've got a chronic complainer. When you've tried the normal recovery approaches and nothing seems to work, look for the following telltale signs:[4]

→ *They always look for someone to blame.* In their world, there is no such thing as an accident: Someone is always at fault, and it's probably you.

→ *They never admit any degree of fault or responsibility.* They see themselves as blameless and victims of the incompetence or malice of others.

→ *They have strong ideas about what others should do.* They love to define other people's duties. If you hear a complaint phrased exclusively in terms of what other people always, never, must, or must not do, chances are you're talking to a chronic complainer.

→ *They complain at length.* While normal complainers pause for breath every now and then, chronic complainers seem able to inhale while saying the words, "And another thing. . . ."

What to Do with This Person

When faced with these occasional chronic complainers (they really are quite rare, fortunately), try these techniques:

- → Actively listen to identify the legitimate grievance beneath the endless griping.
- → Rephrase the complainer's main points in your own words, even if you have to interrupt to do so. You might say something such as, "Excuse me, but do I understand you to say that the service wasn't finished on time and you feel frustrated and annoyed?"
- → Establish the facts to reduce the complainer's tendency to exaggerate or overgeneralize. If the customer says he "tried calling all day, but as usual you tried to avoid me," establish the actual number of times called and when.
- → Resist the temptation to apologize, although that may seem to be the natural thing to do. Since the main thing the complainer is

trying to do is fix blame—not solve problems—your apology will be seen as an open invitation to further blaming. Instead, ask questions such as, "Would an extended warranty solve your problem?" or "When would be the best time for me to call you back with that information?"

→ Force the complainer to pose solutions to the problem, especially if she doesn't seem to like your ideas. Also, try putting a time limit on the conversation by saying something such as, "I have to talk with someone in ten minutes. What sort of action plan can we work out in that time?" Your object is to get the customer to stop whining and to start a problem-solving dialogue with you.

Avoid apologizing to the chronic complainer. An apology will just trigger further complaints.

We have, of course, no guarantees when dealing with such customers, but the effort may well be worth it. Converting one of these folks into a normal, rational customer can be professionally rewarding. If it doesn't work, so be it. You've given your best and that's all anyone can ask.

What You Should Do about Complaint Letters

Customers don't write very often with so many other outlets (e.g., toll-free telephone customer hot lines) available to them today. Nevertheless, or perhaps because they are fairly rare, complaint letters carry considerable impact. Letters provide a graphic and tangible reminder of a customer's dissatisfaction and reflect considerable effort expended. Letter writing isn't easy, so the customer must feel a pretty strong need to go to the trouble.

Letters reflect considerable effort on the customer's part; the letter-writing customer must feel strongly.

If you choose to respond to a letter with a phone call, be certain to have the letter before you and to refer to the specific points as written. Also, make notes of what the customer says and how you respond. If you respond to a letter with a letter of your own, be certain that the letter conveys your attitude of problem solving and projects goodwill and professionalism.

E-mails are less formal than a paper letter, but should be responded to via an e-mail message or a phone call. If you are answering by phone, print a copy of the e-mail to refer to as you speak with the customer.

Be Assertive but Not Abrasive

Assertiveness is absolutely necessary when dealing with customer complaints. But assertiveness is not the same as abrasiveness. Abrasiveness refers to an irritating manner or tone, the kind of writing or talking that sounds pushy or critical. It complicates complaint resolution. To determine if you tend to have an abrasive personality, ask yourself questions such as these:

///
Abrasiveness complicates complaint resolution; assertiveness enhances it.
///

- → Are you often critical of others? When you supervise others, do you speak of "straightening them out" or "whipping them into shape"?
- → Do you have a strong need to be in control? Do you require that almost everything be cleared with you?
- → Are you quick to rise to the attack, to challenge?
- → Do you have a strong need to debate with others? Do your discussions often become arguments?
- → Do you regard yourself as more competent than your peers? Does your behavior let others know that?

The abrasive personality tends to communicate in a manner that can be irritating to others. Try to recognize in yourself the degree to which you have a strong need to control or dominate other people. If you suspect that you have this need, it would be important for you to make an extra effort to soften the tone of your communications.

Assertiveness means being pleasantly direct. Assertive people express their feelings and observations directly and in a manner that is nonthreatening to other people. For example, instead of saying to someone, "You don't make any sense," the assertive person would say, "I'm having a difficult time understanding what you're saying." Or rather than saying, "Deadbeats like you burn me up," the assertive person might say, "People who consistently make late payments cause us a lot of extra work and lost revenue."

//
Assertiveness means being pleasantly direct.
//

Work on being assertive without being abrasive. Assertiveness coupled with the other skills discussed in this chapter can result in holding on to of customers who might otherwise be lost. Developing and using these skills builds customer loyalty and customer capital.

Be Watchful to Catch Complaints before They Happen

Baseball great Yogi Berra used to say, "You can observe a lot by just watching." Customer loyalty builders develop a sense for observing subtle cues that may indicate potential problems with customers. Nonverbal clues can forewarn of small disappointments that can become major complaints.

Do your customers seem to be enjoying themselves when they do business with you? Are they having fun when communicating with your people? Are they appreciating the value of your products and services?

Listen carefully; watch their reactions. Look for the nonverbal indicators of a decrease in satisfaction or a weakening commitment to deal with you. If you suspect waning interest, ask your customers directly if they are still satisfied or if they have ideas on how you can improve your service.

Create a Feedback Log

Create a complaint log. The shortest pencil is better than the longest memory, so get in the habit of jotting down descriptions of complaints received and actions take to resolve them. Use the complaint log as a part of regular staff meetings where you can discuss how the situation has been handled or brainstorm other ways it could be done. The key information you need is shown in Figure 3-1.

Openness to Feedback

The central theme of this chapter is that one of the most critical ingredients in improving your customer's experience is to be receptive to feedback—even from your most severe critics. This, of course, can be painful. But it can also be exceptionally valuable.

Figure 3-1. Sample customer complaint log.

Date/Time	Description of Problem	Value, Systems, or People-Related	Resolution and Follow-Up	Ideas for Avoiding Repeat Problems
June 4, 1 P.M.	Mrs. Jones upset when clerk asked for ID with check	People	Train clerks to not require ID from regular customers.	Program cash registers to ID top customers.
June 12, 7 P.M.	Customer upset when we ran out of widgets; no one around to check stockroom for more product. She had returned especially for it.	Systems	Hand-delivered product to customer 6/13 9 A.M.	Build larger display bins for widgets.
June 13, 10 A.M.	Customer disappointed that widget does not do what he needed it to do.	Value	Provide correct widget; take old one back.	Ask customers how they plan to use widget, and educate about best model for their use.

Feedback Receptiveness Is an Attitude

Less successful businesspeople prefer to be ostriches. They bury their heads and tune out all negative comments. In doing so, they never learn what they need to know to improve. Remember, too, the ostrich always leaves one end exposed.

Think back to the last time you received criticism from someone else. To what degree did you:

> ✦ Hold back on defending or explaining yourself until the full criticism was expressed?
> ✦ Work to understand the speaker's point of view as best you could?
> ✦ Ask for elaboration or clarification?
> ✦ Express an honest reaction?
> ✦ Thank the person for the feedback?

For most people, giving criticism (even in a constructive way) is risky. When customers first offer such feedback, they watch closely to gauge others' responses. The reaction they receive usually determines whether they will offer feedback again. This means that you have an opportunity to avoid turning off future feedback that could be valuable to you.

Tips for Encouraging Continuous Feedback

1. *Don't be defensive.* Listen—don't explain or justify. Learn to withhold your response. When someone is criticizing you, it is not the time to explain or justify your actions, even if you feel the criticism is unwarranted or stems from a misunderstanding. Listen now, explain later. A defensive reaction stifles feedback. It tells others you are more interested in justifying yourself than in understanding what they are saying.

2. *Ask for more information, especially for specifics.* This is a good opportunity to obtain more information. Honest questions will support and encourage the continued flow of feedback. For example, say, "That's very helpful. Tell me more. Is there anything else I should know about?"

3. *Express an honest reaction.* You certainly have a right to express your feelings about the feedback received. You may well say, "I'm a little surprised you said that, but you may have a point," or "I'm not sure what to say. I never even thought of that, but I will from now on."

4. *Thank those providing feedback and plan for the future.* Let people know that you realize how risky giving feedback can be and express your appreciation for their efforts. This might also be a good time to plan for future feedback sessions. These will be less disturbing and more productive than the first one, because you have already demonstrated your receptiveness.

You should realize that few people can handle even these four points, not because they wouldn't benefit from them, but because it takes a lot of courage to seek out and really hear feedback—especially criticism. But the successful loyalty builder is willing to do what the oblivious is not. Getting feedback is a classic example of such an action.

SELF-EVALUATION: FEEDBACK RECEPTIVENESS

Try this feedback receptiveness quiz and use it as a basis for discussion in employee training.

Using a 1 to 5 ranking scale, circle the number that shows the degree to which each of the following statements is true for you.

1 = Almost never true   4 = Often true
2 = Seldom true   5 = Almost always true
3 = Occasionally true

A. I get embarrassed when people point out my mistakes.

    5   4   3   2   1

B. I resent people telling me what they think of my shortcomings.

    5   4   3   2   1

C. I regularly ask friends and associates I trust to comment on how I'm doing.   5   4   3   2   1

D. I know how to offer constructive criticism to others in a sensitive way.

    5   4   3   2   1

E. I like people to tell me their reactions to my activities because it will help me adapt my future behavior.   5   4   3   2   1

If you scored a 4 or 5 on items A and B, you may be putting up some resistance that could deter you from obtaining useful feedback. People are usually uncomfortable when they receive harsh or insensitive feedback, but even that can be useful if we take it in perspective. Even our worst critic can provide a "gift" of good advice if we don't allow emotion to blind us. Successful communicators learn to look for good advice even when it's buried under a lot of worthless noise.

If you answered a 4 or 5 to items C and D, you are creating a climate where helpful feedback is expected and accepted. People who foster such openness can benefit from others' advice.

If you answered a 4 or 5 to item E, you are probably a little unusual. But you're on the right track.

WORKSHEETS:
RECOVERING DISSATISFIED CUSTOMERS

☞ MAKING IT EASY FOR CUSTOMERS TO COMPLAIN

Use this form to brainstorm ideas about how your organization can make it easier for your customers to voice dissatisfaction or complaints. Working alone or with a small group, jot down your ideas for changes without regard for whether they are practical or immediately usable. Then review all ideas for possible adoption by your organization. Put a check-mark next to the ones you want to try.

☐

☐

☐

☐

☐

Develop a priority list of at least two or three items, indicating when you will apply each selected idea. Describe tasks or other resources necessary to implement your ideas.

Prioritized Improvements	*Implementation Requirements*
1.	Time Frame:
	Tasks:
	Task Responsibility:
2.	Time Frame:
	Tasks:
	Task Responsibility:
3.	Time Frame:
	Tasks:
	Task Responsibility:

ACTING UPON CUSTOMER COMPLAINTS

Use this form to brainstorm ideas about how your organization can more effectively act upon customer complaints. Working alone or with a small group, jot down your ideas for changes without regard for whether they are practical or immediately usable. Then review all ideas for possible adoption by your organization. Put a checkmark next to the ones you want to try.

☐
☐
☐
☐
☐

Develop a priority list, indicating when you will apply each selected idea. Describe tasks or other resources necessary to implement your ideas.

Prioritized Improvements	*Implementation Requirements*
1.	Time Frame:
	Tasks:
	Task Responsibility:
2.	Time Frame:
	Tasks:
	Task Responsibility:
3.	Time Frame:
	Tasks:
	Task Responsibility:

Notes

1. Thomas E. Weber, "Can Your Complaints, Adroitly Repackaged, Build a Web Business?" *The Wall Street Journal* (January 10, 2000), p. B1.
2. These U.S. Office of Consumer Affairs statistics are quoted in *The Customer Service Manager's Handbook of People Power Strategies* (Englewood Cliffs, N.J.: Prentice-Hall, 1989), p. 3.
3. R. L. Morgan, *Calming Upset Customers* (Menlo Park, Calif.: Crisp Publications, 1989), p. 40.
4. Adapted from "How to Deal with Those Chronic Complainers," in *Customer Service Manager's Letter,* September 20, 1989, published by Prentice-Hall Professional Newsletters. The article is based on the work of Dr. Robert Bramson, *Coping with Difficult People* (New York: Dell, 1988).

Chapter 4

Strategy 3:
Create Positive Imbalance
with Customers

As a rule, people can get used to anything. If the chances of winning the lottery are a gazillion to one, they don't expect to win—they hope to win. But if their overnight package doesn't arrive, they are seriously aggravated. If the milk they just bought at the store is sour, they're up in arms. If you lead them to believe that they can expect full-on, full-time, no-holds-barred customer service on your website—and they can't—you will have made an enemy where you could have made a friend.
—Jim Sterne, *Customer Service on the Internet*[1]

The Way It Is . . .

A participant at one of my training sessions told me this story: "I have a sister who is nine years younger than I am. When I left home at eighteen, she was still a little girl. She grew up and married a fellow named Travis. They lived 1,000 miles from me. I barely knew Travis. We got together at family parties once every year or two and I'd chat with him for a few moments when I'd call my sister. But our relationship was nothing more than that.

"One day I was in a bookstore and I saw the paperback of Tom Clancy's first book, *The Hunt for Red October*. Well, Travis had been in the nuclear Navy, and I thought he might enjoy this book. So I sprung for the five bucks and got a copy, wrote a little note in it, and sent it to Travis. It wasn't his birthday; it wasn't Christmas. I just felt like sending him a book.

"Well, he was blown over by this. He couldn't believe that someone would do that and he called me immediately and we had a long chat. A few months later, he sent me a videotape on how to improve my golf game.

"The outcome was that we have become quite close. The whole relationship changed because of a simple unexpected gift."

The Role of Balance in Relationships

Human beings are social creatures, constantly going into and out of relationships with others. Some relationships are long-lasting, such as family and lifelong friends. Some relationships are fleeting. They may last for only a few minutes, such as a brief transaction at a service station while traveling cross-country. You may say hello, perhaps chat about the weather, but then you never see that person again.

Social psychology teaches that in all relationships there is a need to establish a balance, a sense of fairness. What we give to the relationship must balance in some way with what we get from it. If we feel we give far more than we receive (or vice versa), we are likely to feel some psychological discomfort.

///
People experience psychological discomfort when relationships are unbalanced.
///

Simple examples of such discomfort might arise when we say hello to someone and they look right at us, but ignore our greeting. Or, in a social situation, imagine that you invite someone to your home for dinner and, after dinner, they leave and never even say thank you. You'd certainly feel some psychological discomfort, perhaps wondering what's wrong with that person—or what's wrong with you.

Knowledge of this psychological phenomenon is useful as we consider the strategy in this chapter: creating positive imbalance with customers. I'll explain why in a moment. First, let's consider why customers act as they do.

At a basic psychological level, people are motivated to act in a particular way because their action will either result in a gain (reward) or avoid a loss (punishment). Customers are rational people. If a buying experience is positive, they will see it as a gain and probably come back; if negative, they'll regard it as a loss and try to avoid returning. If it's so-so, they'll stay in a zone of indifference, being neither motivated nor unmotivated.

The Customer's "Zone of Indifference"

The correlation between customer satisfaction and repeat business (loyalty) can be rather tenuous. Even satisfied customers may be neutral toward their relationship with a business so that some little thing can push them over the edge toward dissatisfaction. Service can meet their needs adequately but fail to motivate their continuing loyalty. Motivation researcher Friedrick Herzberg[2] discovered long ago that satisfied workers are not necessarily motivated workers. Likewise, satisfied customers cannot be assumed to be motivated repeat customers. A "zone of indifference" exists between the satisfied and the motivated. Things are okay, but there is little to tie the customer to the company in the long run. Herzberg argues that satisfaction and motivation are on two different continua. The factors that motivate people are different from the factors that simply prevent dissatisfaction.

Actually, customers who are satisfied may be inert, not motivated. Their satisfaction simply means the absence of dissatisfaction, not the motivation to become a repeat customer. A zone of indifference lies between the dissatisfied and the motivated (see Figure 4-1).

The challenge, then, is to get beyond satisfaction to motivation. This

Figure 4-1. The satisfaction-motivation distinction.

DISSATISFIED ------- SATISFIED ------- MOTIVATED

ZONE OF INDIFFERENCE

is best done by comparing your customers' actual perceptions with what they were expecting in service.

///
The challenge is to get customers out of their zone of indifference and motivate them to become loyal.
///

The Crucial Role of Customer Anticipation

As customers enter into a transaction, they anticipate (albeit perhaps unconsciously) a certain kind of experience; they expect to be treated a particular way. What they anticipate is often based on their past associations with this business, person, or organization, or with other experiences that they see as similar. If they had a good experience in the past, they'll probably anticipate something satisfactory. If the last transaction wasn't so positive, they might assume the next one won't be better.

What customers anticipate is *perceptual*. It exists in the customer's mind. Sometimes these perceptions are accurate and rational, sometimes they aren't. And to make matters even more challenging for a service provider, perceptions are ever-changing, presenting a moving, hard-to-define target.

///
We cannot predict with absolute certainty what a customer anticipates because such anticipation is perceptual and unique to that individual.
///

Anticipating the Core Product or Service

When people judge the quality of a tangible product, they use fairly objective and somewhat predictable standards. For example, if you are buying a new automobile, you'll likely judge its quality using criteria such as:

- → The car's driving and handling characteristics
- → Low frequency of repair (i.e., the car seldom has to be fixed)
- → Appropriate size (i.e., the car holds my family comfortably)
- → Price relative to its quality (i.e., the car is a good value for the price)

+ Workmanship (i.e., the car seems to be well built and has a nice paint job)

Likewise when judging the quality of a service—say, a house painter's job—people will measure it by such standards as whether:

+ The work was done on time (i.e., the painter met the deadline).
+ The surfaces to be painted were carefully prepared.
+ The paints were mixed and applied neatly.
+ The painter cleaned up after the job.

These kinds of standards are relatively predictable; they are much the same for each customer.

But evaluating the degree of customer satisfaction goes beyond the core product or service bought. It involves the entire buying experience. The standards by which customers measure overall satisfaction are more ambiguous.

SELF-EVALUATION: IDENTIFY CORE ANTICIPATIONS

What must happen for you to maintain a basic level of customer satisfaction during the purchase of a product or service? Identify your core anticipations for each of the following purchases. Be specific about what you'd consider to be basic anticipations:

A washing machine
A computer system
Repair service for your automobile's transmission
Lawn service for your home
Copy service for an important report
A new bicycle
A dental checkup
A complete physical
Carpet cleaning

(Note: Later in this chapter you'll be asked to revisit the basic anticipations you identify here.)

Anticipating the Whole Buying Experience

What customers anticipate about the core product is only part of the mental process they go through. People will anticipate different experiences among different organizations or under differing circumstances. For example, they could buy the same core product but from several different places. They are likely to anticipate different treatment from a "high-touch," full-service retailer than they do from a warehouse store. They would anticipate different service from a prestigious law firm and a state auto license bureau. They might well anticipate different experiences from a well-known technology firm's sales representative as compared to a catalog distributor's website. For that matter, people often anticipate something different from the same store at different times. Perhaps a little less personal attention is anticipated during busy periods such as the Christmas season or end-of-month license plate deadline times.

Factoring in Different Anticipations from Different Businesses

Suppose you intend to shop at a low-cost, self-service, discount store such as a Kmart, Target, or Fred Meyers. Going into the store, you anticipate being treated in a particular way. You do not necessarily expect the clerk in the clothing department (if you can find one) to be an expert in fitting clothing, or to be particularly helpful in color-coordinating items. This is not to say that some people who work there would not have these skills, but you probably wouldn't anticipate them as a general rule.

If you simply select some clothing items and take them to a checkout for purchase, you are not surprised or disappointed—you expected unassisted self-service. The experience is what you anticipated and, if other aspects of the store are acceptable (e.g., it seems clean and well stocked), you may be perfectly satisfied.

By contrast, if you go to a Nordstrom, Macy's, or Bloomingdale's full-service department store, or to an exclusive boutique, you would anticipate a different kind of transaction. You would probably expect salespeople to have considerable expertise in clothing fit, color, and materials. You would realistically anticipate clerks to give you full attention and assistance as you make your purchases.

When you experience situations such as those just described, what you anticipated was validated—you get about what you expected. Dissatisfaction is probably avoided; you are likely to be in the zone of indifference.

Using What Customers Anticipate to Build Loyalty

Getting customers beyond the zone of indifference is the goal. The key to motivating a customer to feel loyalty, however, lies not in meeting what the customer anticipates but in exceeding it. To do this, you need to have some conception of what the customer anticipates. How can you best anticipate changing customer needs?

Staying Close to Customers Clarifies What They Anticipate

Nothing is more important than staying close to your customers and maintaining an ongoing dialogue. To do so requires every company member to be a sensing device, a curious information gatherer.

//
To understand customer anticipations means staying in close contact with the customer.
//

Three things are necessary for ongoing customer sensing:

> → Employees who are taught to get customer feedback, and are rewarded for it
> → Processes for harvesting and using customer feedback
> → Empowered employees who respond to customer feedback in productive ways

What can you do with the input received from customers? You can use it to best understand what they anticipate when doing business with your organization. Customer perceptions are exceptionally valuable data. Only when we have a sense of what is anticipated can we exceed expectations and thus build customer loyalty. Ultimately, today's customer service success arises from a central theme that is simple to state yet challenging to implement. The underlying theme is:

You achieve customer satisfaction, retention, and loyalty by exceeding in positive ways what customers anticipate.

The Concept of A-Plus

We'll call this process of exceeding the anticipated the A-plus strategy. Research and the experiences of countless experts point to A-plus as the "master key" to service success.

As customers compare what they anticipate with the service received, one of three situations will show up:

1. The experience was not as positive (or was more negative) than the customer anticipated.
2. The experience largely matched what the customer anticipated.
3. The experience was more positive (or less negative) than the customer anticipated.

In situation number 1, the customer's experience was not very good. She's dissatisfied and likely to defect to another provider, if she has a rational alternative.

In situation number 2, the customer is neither dissatisfied nor particularly motivated to return. This is the zone of indifference we discussed previously.

In situation number 3, the transaction was better than anticipated. Either the customer thought it would be acceptably good and it turned out to be very good, or the customer thought it would not be particularly good but it wasn't as bad as anticipated. If positive anticipations were sufficiently exceeded (or negative ones were shown to be unfounded), this customer is a prime candidate for repeat business.

Situation number 3 is what we'll call an A-plus experience—customer anticipations were exceeded in positive ways.

Why A-Plus Leads to Customer Retention

A theory from the field of social psychology called equity theory provides a solid theoretical basis for predicting that the A-plus customer will become a repeat customer. Psychologist J. Stacy Adams first articulated this theory in the mid-1960s. It has stood the test of time to be widely accepted as a predictor of some kinds of human behavior.

A Brief Description of Equity Theory

Equity theory starts with the premise I described earlier—that human beings constantly go into and out of various kinds of relationships, ranging from the intimate to the cursory. The buyer-seller relationship is germane to this discussion.

Once in a relationship, even a brief one, people regularly assess the relative equity or fairness of their involvement compared to other people. They check to see if what they give to the relationship seems appropriate to what they are getting out of it. A very simple example of a relationship that is out of balance (i.e., inequitable) would arise if you gave something (e.g., a tangible gift, a greeting, a special favor) and received nothing in return.

Inequitable relationships feel awkward and often uncomfortable. Common courtesy demands that we do something to "rebalance" the relationship. When invited to dinner, people strive to rebalance by bringing a dish to share at the meal, or they may bring the host or hostess a gift. Or the guest invites the host or hostess to an event. This behavior is ingrained in the social mores of most cultures. People who take but never give are soon found lonely.

Much of the early testing of this theory focused on the workplace, where workers' perceptions of fairness (i.e., equity) were correlated with certain behaviors. Not surprisingly, studies found that people who were paid less for doing the same work as others, for example, felt a sense of inequity. In my own doctoral dissertation, I found that employees who sensed that their supervisor communicated more often and more positively with other employees in the workgroup felt a clear sense of inequity.[3]

The theory goes beyond simply citing situations where people may feel inequitably treated. It also predicts what people are likely to do about it. When inequity is perceived, people will respond with one or some combination of the following reactions:

➔ *Ignoring or Rationalizing the Inequity.* The offended person makes up a reason. For example, "He deserves to be treated better than me,"

"The world isn't fair, but I'm not going to fight it," or "I guess he didn't hear me say hello."

↦ *Demanding Restitution.* The offended person goes to the boss to demand fairer pay, or the customer wants her money back when product quality is poor.

↦ *Retaliating.* The offended person tells others about how bad the organization is, attempts to do harm to the person seen as the cause of the inequity, or engages in outright sabotage.

↦ *Withdrawing from the Relationship.* The offended person quits the relationship and doesn't come back.

So far this theory seems to bear out common sense. If we feel we are being unfairly treated, we get upset and usually do something about it. Hence, the unsatisfied participant in a relationship (the customer in our case) is likely to have one of these reactions. The first two alternatives may give you, as a business, a chance to patch things up and retain the customer using recovery techniques such as those learned in Chapter 3. But the last two responses—retaliation or withdrawal—can be devastating. Mrs. Williams, the former Happy Jack's Super Market customer in our Chapter 2 story, did both. She withdrew (i.e., quit shopping at the store) and retaliated by telling her friends to boycott the store, thus starting the negative ripple effects that may have resulted in scores or even hundreds of lost customers or potential customers.

The Positive Side of Equity Theory

Here is where the theory gets even more interesting: People who feel that they are receiving more than they "deserve" from a transaction also experience a psychological need to restore the balance of fairness. A simple illustration of this is the psychological pressure you may feel to reciprocate when someone does something unusually nice for you. The relationship will remain unbalanced until you rebalance it with a similar kindness or some other positive action.

Herein lies the theoretical basis for our A-plus strategy for exceeding customer anticipations. By going beyond what people anticipate, you create an imbalance that, for many people, requires action on their part to rebalance. The logical options are the opposite of what the victim of a negative imbalance feels: The individual could rationalize or ignore it, of course, but attempts to restore the balance could also take the form of telling others of the positive experience, paying a premium for the goods received, or, in short, becoming a loyal customer.

The challenge, then, is to create positive imbalances by exceeding what customers anticipate. This is the master key to creating an A-plus strategy for building customer loyalty and growing customer capital.

//

The A-plus strategy is rooted in equity theory—the use of positive imbalance to motivate customer loyalty.

//

Putting the A-Plus Strategy to Work

Putting the A-plus strategy to work requires two ongoing actions:

1. Continuously working to anticipate what customers anticipate
2. Exceeding what the customer anticipates

There are three ways to get a sharper picture of what the customer anticipates when doing business with you: persistently fishing for feedback, using focus groups, and using explorer groups.

Fishing for Feedback with Naive Listening

The best way to fish for feedback as an everyday activity is with "naive" listening. Naive listening is more of an attitude than a strategy. As its name implies, this kind of listening conveys that you don't know (i.e., are naive) about what the customer wants. Your task is to get them to explain it to you. Create an atmosphere where you and your people are cheerfully receptive to customer comments, even—nay, especially—comments that may not be pleasant to hear.

As we discussed in Chapter 3, the best way to collect feedback is to make it easy for your customers to complain. Let customers know that you are receptive to their comments, problems, or concerns. Then provide ways for them to tell you what's on their minds.

For example, one effective technique is the use of open-ended questions. An open-ended question is one that cannot be answered with a simple yes, no, or other one-word response. As such, people must invariably convey much more information. Restaurant servers who ask, "How else can I make your dinner enjoyable?" will get a broader range of responses than one who asks, "Do you need anything else?" or "Is everything okay?"

Use open-ended questions to get more complete information.

Of course, questions aren't just for the complainer. We also need to know what changes we need to make to maintain our better customers' ever-changing anticipations. Here is where the focus group comes in.

Using Focus Groups

Focus groups have long been used for marketing research, but they can also play an exceptionally important role in understanding customer perceptions and expectations.

Although some marketing consultants may disagree with me, there's no great mystery to how focus groups work, and any intelligent person can run one effectively (for more information, see the sidebar Another Look: How to Run a Focus Group).

Focus groups, long used for marketing research, can tell you much about what customers anticipate.

Using Explorer Groups

Exploration involves going to other businesses to see how they do things. When you hear about a great idea that another business is using, send out an explorer group to scope it out. One retailer known for exceptional service encourages employees to take a company van and rush to the scene of good service given by others. They take notes and discuss possible implementation in their own store. Explorer groups need not be sent

//

Another Look: How to Run a Focus Group

Here is the procedure for creating a focus group:

→ *Select a sample of your customers or patrons to join with you in the focus group session.* Don't just pick people you know or customers you like. You may, however, want to be sure they are among your better customers by qualifying them according to their influence or how much they spend with you. You can get customer names off their checks or credit cards or whatever other records you have.

→ *Formally invite the customers to participate.* Tell them when and where as well as how long the session will take. Let them know the purpose for the focus group: that you are attempting to better understand customer needs and how you can better be of service to them.

→ *Limit your focus group to not less than five or more than a dozen people.* Ask customers to confirm their attendance, but expect that some will not show up. Fifteen confirmed reservations will generally get you twelve actual participants. Follow up with phone calls to confirm attendance. (One supermarket chain was so excited about the focus groups that they invited forty or fifty people every month. The problem, of course, is that a group that large made it difficult for all people to be heard. Some people dominated the group while others, who had equally good ideas but were uncomfortable speaking before so many people, suppressed their ideas.)

→ *Reward focus group participants.* Tell those invited that you will give them something for their participation. Retail stores may give focus group participants a gift certificate, a free dinner, or even cash. In marketing research, it's not uncommon to pay people $50 or more for a one- or two-hour session.

To get the most from focus groups, try these best practices:

→ Set the stage by having someone from top management moderate the group.

→ Create an open atmosphere where participants can feel comfortable giving you all kinds of feedback. Be polite, open, encouraging, and receptive.

↬ Avoid cutting people off when they're making a critical comment, and, above all, do not be defensive of the way you're doing business now, when in the eyes of the customer it's not working.

↬ Keep any follow-up questions open-ended. Don't interrogate.

↬ As focus group members express compliments, acknowledge them and thank people for the favorable comments. Then make a statement such as, "We're happy to hear that we are doing things you like, but our major purpose here is to identify ways that we can do a better job in meeting your needs. How can we do even better?"

↬ Limit the group to a predetermined amount of time; typically a one-hour or (maximum) ninety-minute session works best. Any longer than that and you start losing people's interest.

↬ Tape-record the entire focus group session and transcribe key notes for review. As you analyze the results of this group session, look for keywords that may tip you off to what the customers are looking for. If, for example, concerns about the amount of time needed to complete a transaction come up repeatedly, you can start to compile ideas on how you might meet customer needs more quickly.

↬ At the end of the focus group session, of course, be sure to thank the participants for all of their input—and give them their pay.

only to direct competitors; often totally unrelated businesses have great ideas you can use.

Another way to gather great data is to "explore" how your own organization is serving customers by being a customer. If you are a manager, anonymously call the company and listen to the impression created by the person answering the phone. Is this what your customer is hearing? How do you like it? Then visit other locations or areas in your own organization and see how you are treated.

Regularly explore other company's ideas as well as how you are being perceived by your own customers.

Go fishing for feedback regularly. Use ongoing naive listening, focus groups, and explorer groups to assess your business and your competition through the eyes of your customers. Open the communication channels and give your customer an opportunity to comment and complain. Customers who have their complaints heard and handled are very likely to do business with the company again. U.S. Office of Consumer Affairs research shows that as few as 9 percent of dissatisfied customers *who do not complain about their service problems* report a willingness to do business with the same company again. However, as many as 80 percent of those whose complaints were resolved will consider doing repeat business—even if their complaints were not fully resolved in their favor[4]. In a sense, your complaining customer is your best customer. Meeting his or her needs provides an opportunity to solidify a business relationship.

SELF-EVALUATION: SET GREATER EXPECTATIONS

Take a look at your responses to the Self-Evaluation: Identify Core Anticipations. In that exercise, you identified core expectations about various products or services, or the basics needed to keep you satisfied. Now think about going beyond these basics. What might be some unanticipated surprises that you could receive from an enlightened business applying an A-plus strategy? What "little things" could make you much more likely to become a loyal customer?

Understanding customer anticipations does little good unless you take the second step in the A-plus process: regularly developing ways to exceed anticipations.

Exceeding What Customers Anticipate

Now let's apply this A-plus idea to a familiar retailing situation we have all experienced. Think about shopping at a large discount retailer like Kmart, Target, or Fred Meyers. How might the retailer exceed what you anticipate—that is, provide some level of service above and beyond what you'd normally expect?

Suppose, for example, you found a person greeting you at the door as you entered the store. Suppose that person welcomed you to the store and asked if they can help you find anything in particular. Would that be just a little more than you have anticipated? Perhaps so, but that is, of course, precisely what Wal-Mart stores have done. By hiring people to serve as greeters, often senior citizens on a part-time basis, Wal-Mart surprises its discount store shoppers and, in the process, puts a human face on a giant corporation.

Incidentally, Wal-Mart founder Sam Walton was a believer in surprising customers with little things. Both Wal-Mart and Kmart were founded in 1962. Kmart grew out of an existing retailer called S. S. Kresge, an old-line five-and-dime store chain. Walton's strategy called for developing discount stores in small towns, initially concentrating on southern states. Kmart expanded more rapidly than Wal-Mart during the early years.

The outgrowth of the different expansion strategies is that shoppers largely developed their anticipations of discount retailing based on their experience in Kmart stores. All Walton had to do was take the Kmart expectation and exceed it in the customer's eyes. The use of in-store greeters was one way to A-plus Kmart shoppers and convert them into Wal-Mart shoppers.

Additionally, Walton was a big believer in employee autonomy and creativity. If Wal-Mart employees had an idea for promoting a particular product, for example, they were encouraged to try it. Kmart used more centralized decision making, often requiring approval from corporate offices for even minor innovations. Walton's employees were more empowered to innovate for their customers.

The idea that little things can make huge differences is illustrated by the Wal-Mart–Kmart comparison. So much is the same, yet the results are dramatically different.

The "little things principle" is dramatically illustrated by comparing these two retail giants. While the two have about the same number and size of stores, sell essentially the same products, and offer comparable prices and equally convenient locations, Wal-Mart has done a better job in exceeding customer anticipations with little things. Corporate performance differences are staggering: Wal-Mart sales have climbed to more than $160 billion in 1999, whereas Kmart remains stuck where it's been for several years at about a quarter of that revenue figure. Wal-Mart's stock price grew six-fold during the 1990s while Kmart's has stayed mired in the $10 to $18 range. Much of the differential, I believe, is because Wal-Mart has done a better job of using little things to A-plus its customers.

But wait, the greeter idea has been done. Yesterday's breakthrough idea can be easily imitated. That is why the A-plus strategy provides a way to continuously raise the bar. Already tried the greeter? Are there ways we can take this idea a step further? For example, the store could hire employees to roam the store aisles wearing vests that say "Can I Help You Find Something?" and look for customers who appear to be confused or overwhelmed. This employee would also be exceptionally personable and know a lot about the products in the store. Wouldn't that exceed what most people anticipate in a self-service store? Home Depot and Lowes Hardware provide such a service. These are simple examples of A-plus actions, of consistently doing little things that surprise the customer.

In the remainder of this book I will describe strategies for applying the A-plus principle of creating positive imbalances with customers. These strategies can be taught to all employees and can provide a basis for a coherent, ongoing strategy for constantly improving customer service in ways that will increase loyalty and build customer capital. By applying these straightforward strategies consistently, your organization can create an ever-evolving paradigm for achieving new levels of service and customer loyalty. The payoff is enormous.

WORKSHEET: CREATING POSITIVE IMBALANCE

✍ RECOGNIZING THE IMPACT OF INEQUITY IN RELATIONSHIPS

Think back on several relationships (either long-term or brief) that you have experienced. Using the form that's provided here, name the relationship and then compare what you gave to that relationship with what you got from it. To what extent do you feel that the exchange is equitable and fair?

Relationship	What I Give	What I Get	Fairness?
1. _____	_____	_____	_____
2. _____	_____	_____	_____
3. _____	_____	_____	_____
4. _____	_____	_____	_____

Notes

1. Jim Sterne, *Customer Service on the Internet* (New York: John Wiley & Sons, 1996), p. 46.
2. F. Herzberg, B. Mausner, and B. Snyderman, *The Motivation to Work*, 2nd ed. (New York: Wiley, 1959).
3. Paul R. Timm, "Effects of Inequity in Supervisory Communication Behavior on Subordinates in Clerical Workgroups," unpublished doctoral dissertation, Florida State University, 1977.
4. These U.S. Office of Consumer Affairs statistics are quoted in *The Customer Service Manager's Handbook of People Power Strategies* (Englewood Cliffs, N.J.: Prentice-Hall, 1989), p. 3.

Chapter 5

Strategy 4: Give Customers A-Plus Value

Unless companies want to be in a commoditized business,
they will be compelled to upgrade their offerings to the next
stage of economic value.
— B. Joseph Pine and James H. Gilmore[1]

The Way It Is . . .

You can find exceptional value in some unusual places. A *Wall Street Journal* article once sang the praises of the public toilets in Suwon, South Korea. The city is so proud of its exceptional toilet facilities that it gives weekly tours to tourists to show them off. The public rest room is inside a building with the sloping wooden roof of a traditional Korean pavilion. Guests are invited to try out the "heated toilet seats, examine the sinks, and take pictures. . . . Violin music plays in the background, and small paintings of the Korean countryside hang on the walls. . . . The facilities have bouquets of flowers—both fake and genuine—automatic faucets, sliding stall doors for the disabled, and solar-powered heat. Speakers pipe in Vivaldi's 'Four Seasons,' Korean palace music, or recordings of chirping birds."[2]

The perception of value is highly subjective, but people seem to know it when they experience it. While long-term durability or utility is often seen as the ultimate value, companies can't always wait for their customers to recognize this. What companies can do is focus on creating an enhanced *sense* of customer value.

A-Plus Value: What It Is

We talked in Chapter 2 about value as one of the three categories of customer turnoffs. In this chapter, we consider perceptions of value as one way to create an A-plus, loyalty-building experience. We can build customer loyalty by giving customers an enhanced sense of value—something that exceeds what they anticipate. But what, exactly, is a sense of value?

A basic definition of value is product quality relative to its cost. If you purchase a cheap throwaway product, say, an inexpensive disposable camera that costs less than $10, and the pictures are not quite up to studio quality, you probably wouldn't be overly upset. You expected snapshots, not professional portraits. If, however, you spend $900 for a deluxe camera with many professional-quality features and the pictures are little better than those produced by the disposable camera, you'd have a right to be upset. As well you should be.

Likewise, if you give a kid a few dollars to mow your lawn and he doesn't get it exactly right, you chalk it up to a learning experience. But if you hire an expensive lawn care professional and the work isn't up to snuff, you are likely to get upset. You anticipate getting what you pay for; the more you pay, the more you expect.

In the case of our opening story, the cost of the public rest room is nil and the experience far exceeds what customers would ever anticipate. The payoff in this case is public pride and civic satisfaction, as well as possible new tourists.

//

Letting customer perceptions of value slide leads to devastating effects for companies. Successful organizations must keep in tune with their customers' perceptions of value.

//

How to Create an Enhanced Sense of Value

The perception of value is based on individual views of intrinsic and extrinsic or associated factors. Understanding these factors is the starting point for creating A-plus value experiences for your customers.

//

Sometimes even good companies let their quality slip and customers eventually catch on. In the 1980s and early 1990s, Volkswagen Corporation of America saw its car sales drop by 90 percent to less than 50,000 in 1993, compared to its 1970 high of over a half-million cars sold. What happened?

Much of VW's competitive advantage in subcompact cars evaporated when competitors (especially the Japanese manufacturers) engaged in extended conversations with their customers and used feedback received to develop appealing features. While VW engineers "knew the right way" to position a steering wheel, Japanese manufacturers offered adjustable tilt wheels. While VW was certain that its radios were "just fine," competitors responded to customer desires for multispeaker stereo sound. The result: Customers perceived VW as offering less value. By the early 1990s, Volkswagen of America was fighting for its life. Fortunately for VW, the late 1990s brought a significant turnaround and the company is thriving. But it almost didn't make it after having paid a terrible price for not staying current with customer expectations and wants.

While A-plus value builds customer loyalty, its opposite—the failure to meet changing perceptions of value—can destroy a company. It is noteworthy that VW learned from this experience and has produced a remarkable turnaround. By the mid-1990s the company regained its traditional position as one of the most innovative and successful auto manufacturers.

//

Intrinsic Value of the Product Itself

Intrinsic value of a product may not become evident for a long time. You don't fully appreciate the value until the truck has 100,000 miles on it, or the legal document your attorney prepared holds up in court, or the house-painting job still looks great years later. For example, "Hotel Room Scrunch!" was the headline of a *Wall Street Journal* story on the diminished Intrinsic value in hotel rooms. The story cited sixteen hotels that are actively building smaller and smaller rooms while still charging premium rates. The smallest rooms were found at the Paramount in New York. They had only 101 square feet! Some hotels were offering up to 75 percent of their rooms in the under 225-square-foot range (*The Wall Street Journal,* January 21, 2000).

In my training sessions, I often ask participants to talk about products or services that have exceeded what they anticipated in terms of intrinsic value. People often respond by mentioning exceptionally reliable products such as Toyota automobiles and trucks,[3] Kirby vacuum cleaners, certain appliances, and Craftsman tools, to name a few examples. We can all think of something we have owned that has lasted a long time and earned our brand loyalty. These products consistently exceed what we have anticipated in terms of value.

Value takes on another look for intangible products or for services. With these products, accuracy and attention to detail of the product provider may be the hallmark of value. A utility, cable provider, or financial institution that gives customers consistently accurate, easy-to-read statements may be giving A-plus service. The company that makes it easy for customers to contact its representatives, and then responds quickly to fix any errors or problems, will be perceived by customers as high in value.

The opposite creates immediate and often lasting negative pictures of value. One day in the summer of 1999, the phones stopped working at the national reservation center of LOT Polish Airlines in New York. The airline called the telephone company's problem line at 9 A.M. Eleven hours later, after the reservations center had closed for the day, a repairman arrived. Before all was fixed, the center was without phone service for thirty-three hours (*The Wall Street Journal,* January 19, 2000). The intrinsic value was clearly lacking.

Of the many credit cards I carry, my favorites are the American Express Card and Discover Private Issue. I perceive higher intrinsic value in these products for two reasons: They give me airline miles or cash back, and when I need to call either of these providers I can speak to a live person almost immediately. Other cards linger in my wallet because, when I have a problem, they force me through a maze of telephone switching that is annoying and time-consuming. This live-person contact enhances my perception of intrinsic value.

Still another example of intrinsic value is provided to key customers by some private banking clients—whether individuals or corporations—who receive the personal touch. Each client is assigned to a bank executive willing to meet personally with the client to oversee his or her financial needs.

///

Successful companies constantly look for ways to enhance customers' perceptions of value. This is especially important for their key customers.

///

Extrinsic or Associated Value

Extrinsic or associated value goes beyond the core product. It involves more than whether or not an automobile starts and runs reliably or the degree to which an Internet service provider stays up and running. It involves the entire customer relationship.

Remember that value is perceptual. Since perception, by definition, is different for different individuals, some people may be turned on by a company's enhanced value efforts while others may regard them as nothing more than what is expected, or worse, as fluff.

The challenge is to create conditions that improve the likelihood of favorable perceptions. Companies may seek to enhance the perception of value through:

- Packaging
- Guarantees and warranties
- Goodness of product fit
- Memorability of product experience
- Uniqueness and shared values
- Company credibility
- Add-ons

Build A-Plus Value with Packaging

You go to a hardware store to buy a power drill. There you find a stack of the model you want. All but one of the drills is in its original package. What is the likelihood that you would select the one without a box? Zero, right? You will undoubtedly buy one in a box even knowing that you'll throw the box away when you get home. The box—the package—enhances the value.

A business associate of mine occasionally gives me books he thinks will be useful in my consulting and training work. Sometimes, he simply hands me a copy of a recommended book. On a few occasions, he enhanced the value of his gift by:

+ Writing a friendly note in the book
+ Referring me to a particular section he thinks will be especially useful
+ Using a silver ink pen to write the note
+ Gift-wrapping the book

The product is the same—it's the packaging and personalization that enhance my sense of its value. This illustrates the "little things" principle introduced in Chapter 4. Tiny differences make the extrinsic value of the product greater.

While working in Iceland recently, I shopped for some Icelandic wool gifts for my daughters. After receiving adequate but nondescript service in several shops, I found one store in Reykjavik called Vik Wool that had particularly friendly employees and a nice selection of knitted gloves. I selected two pairs and a few other small items. When the clerk rang up my goods, she wrapped each gift in a small hand-knit sack tied with a ribbon. The little sacks were made of knitting remnants from their factory. The packaging of these inexpensive gifts far exceeded what I had anticipated. Other stores set the expectation with generic plastic bags; Vik Wool A-plusses customers with the beautiful knitted wool sacks.

If your business sells intangibles, don't overlook possible packaging. If anything, packing enhancements can be even more powerful when they are completely unexpected. Packaging the intangible adds extrinsic value to the product. But how do we package an intangible?

A successful insurance sales representative I know gives his clients their policies in an attractive leather portfolio that can be used to store other important papers. He goes a step further by engraving the client's name on the portfolio. To this day I have such a leather binder given me almost twenty years ago. Heck, it has my name engraved on it. Who else would want it?

If your customers receive only documents in exchange for their money (the only tangible product associated with a service), give some thought to packaging these papers in an attractive or useful manner. Or add some tangible items that might relate to your services. AirTouch Cellular sent its best customers a "road travel gift set." It included a thermos, a bag of Starbucks coffee, and some snacks.

Upscale department stores have long known the value of attractive gift-wrapping. Customers love it. Especially customers like me who are all thumbs when it comes to wrapping gifts.

These are just a few specific examples, but any organization can enhance its packaging and thus increase the customer's perception of value.

///
Packaging is important from both a marketing and customer service perspective. It can be especially useful when it surprises the customer.
///

Build A-Plus Value with Guarantees and Warranties

Would you be likely to see a product with a "lifetime warranty" as having higher value than a similar product with a thirty-day warranty? Most people do. I used to tell customers who purchased my videotape training programs that these were unconditionally guaranteed for thirty days. If they felt the programs did not meet their needs, they could return the videos within thirty days and get a full refund. Then I began to think about enhancing this sense of value and changed that guarantee to forever. If ever the customer felt the product did not meet his or her needs, it could be returned for a full refund.

I found that with the unlimited guarantee period, the percent of goods returned was unchanged. In fact, with the thirty-day guarantee, I may actually have been encouraging refund requests by setting a target date. The customer who has had the product for twenty-five days or so may have felt some urgency to make a decision, and that decision might be to send the product back. A lifetime guarantee eliminates the motivation to act now, reducing the likelihood the customer will return the product.

If your product has good intrinsic value, the return rates for short-term guarantees versus long-term or lifetime guarantees will be virtually equal.

Nordstrom department stores have earned a tremendous amount of good publicity because of its no-questions-asked, unconditional return policy. The oft-repeated story of the fellow who returned a set of tires to

Nordstrom's (which doesn't sell tires, of course) has had an incredibly positive ripple effect. The tale has become legend and, when written about in Tom Peters and Robert Waterman's 1982 best-seller *In Search of Excellence,* caught the eye of millions of readers, many of whom are exactly the kind of customer Nordstrom caters to. The cost of granting the request of one unreasonable customer bought incalculable advertising.

Ironically, in some countries, government regulation forbids lifetime guarantees. The American catalog company, Lands' End, has a simple and reassuring motto for its shoppers that says: GUARANTEED. PERIOD. Some shortsighted competitors took Lands' End to court in Germany. They claimed this was unfair advertising and got the court to agree that this guarantee policy was "economically unfeasible" and therefore amounted to unfair competition.

That is a classic case of thinking small and not understanding the value of A-plus service. Lands' End responded to the court ruling with a set of ads in German newspapers and magazines poking fun at the ban. One ad pictures a fly with the caption, "One-day guarantee." Another showed a washing machine, guaranteed six months. Other companies facing similar bans (e.g., Zippo lighters, Tupperware) have dropped their lifetime guarantees but are benefiting from the publicity. Zippo ran ads in British papers proclaiming, "A Guarantee So Good the Germans Banned It."[4]

//

Surprise your customers with an unusually generous warranty or guarantee.

//

Your company can quibble over guarantees or take advantage of A-plus value perceptions by being generous and open. Consider calculating the occasional unreasonable customer who takes unfair advantage of a generous guarantee as a cost of doing business. Pleasantly surprise the large majority of your customers by offering generous guarantee terms. Go beyond what the customer anticipates and reap the reward of customer loyalty.

Build A-Plus Value with Goodness of Product Fit

A good friend of mine works as a senior knowledge engineer for a company that sells intelligent systems software to manage customer relationships. This CRM software crunches an enormous amount of data and gives its user specific recommendations for personalizing customer contacts. I can best explain this with a hypothetical example.

Suppose that you are in a financial services business such as a consumer bank or credit union. Using this software, a customer who calls or visits your office would deal with a person who knows a great deal about him. George Customer calls your office with a question about his mortgage. Your employee would key in the customer's account number. The intelligent systems would display a series of dialogues your employee could use—word for word—to explain customer options and perhaps sell additional products.

The software system gathers and digests mountains of data about the individual customer and about people like him (i.e., demographic data). The system may have information about how many cars this customer owns and their price range. It may also factor in other personal information about George. For example, he is fifty-five years old, recently divorced, and has grown kids; his mortgage is almost paid off, his Oldsmobile is four years old, and he recently changed jobs after receiving a substantial payout from his previous employer. If you were a financial institution, would you want to have such information? I would.

All this data can suggest additional products your business could sell to George. And, in doing so, your business can use this information to build a stronger relationship and provide A-plus value by offering products that fit perfectly with this customer's needs. Obviously your business, too, benefits.

One large mortgage company that uses this advanced contact management system has had tremendous success in increasing the close rate for additional products. Previously, 4 percent of customers contacting the company purchased additional products. After implementing the system, which provides explicit prompts for customer representatives, the close rate jumped to 38 percent.[5]

The benefit of such additional sales is obvious, but the customer service element is equally important. This marriage of technology and customer contact builds relationships, enhances customer loyalty, and ultimately builds customer capital.

One word of caution: Some people fear that gathering and using such information may be a violation of personal privacy. Abuses of personal information could result in a customer backlash or even government actions to protect consumers from unreasonable intrusions. Be certain that company systems gather only appropriate information.

Sophisticated customer relationship management products are becoming less expensive and more readily available. Even small businesses can learn about customer needs, wants, and preferences by gathering appropriate personal data and monitoring demographic trends. In doing so, they are able to A-plus their value to customers.

Goodness of fit means thinking one-size-fits-one. Personalization, not classification into demographic groups, permits real relationship building. A January 1998 issue of *Fortune* ran a letter to the editor written by a thirteen-year-old girl who "often enjoys reading [the] magazine." She was responding to an article called "Girl Power!" in which the magazine described what girls her age were into. The young lady's articulate response explained that she was not at all like the profile offered in the article. She also criticized *Seventeen, YM, Teen,* and the other magazines that think "much the way you do: that girls can be broken down into a demographic group, that our minds consist of very little more than boys, shopping, makeup, boys, clothes, and shopping."

She went on to say, "My request to you is that if you are going to say things like this, don't. There is no movie that all girls like, there is no way we all like to dress, there is no music we all like to listen to. It's never fair to make generalizations about any group of people, be it teenage girls or middle-aged businesspeople. Sorry to break it to you, but I am not a demographic group and I don't like your stereotypes, and that is Girl Power!"[6]

Mass customization is becoming a hallmark of manufacturing. Companies are creating products just the way the customer wants them. Levi's can customize jeans to the exact measurements of individual customers. Most companies can offer menus of product characteristics for customer to select from. Companies can create "industrial intimacy" by listening very carefully to the customer's input and customizing products to that customer. Progressive banks, for example, invite customers to select the terms of their consumer loans and home mortgages and immediately responds with customized interest rates and fees. Ultimately, the key is to focus on what is important to the customer and, as long as this still permits the company to make a profit, give the customer exactly what she wants.

The Internet is a popular medium for custom orders. Ford Motor

Co. lets buyers "build a vehicle" from a palette of options, while Golf to Fit crafts custom clubs based on questionnaire responses. The average person can buy custom clothing at an affordable price, made-to-order music CDs, even personalized vitamins, on the Net. Many economists believe that if you don't mass customize, you're going to lose business in today's marketplace.[7]

///
To provide A-plus value, your company needs to be implementing one-to-one customer service.
///

No one wants to be a number or a piece of demographic data. People have individual needs and wants and must be treated as unique. A-plus value is personalized value. It is doing all you can to be sure the products or services you offer fit the needs of the individual customer, not just some large demographic group.

Build A-Plus Value with Memorable Experiences

A highlight of my kid's birthday celebrations have been trips to Chuck E. Cheese restaurants. Well, maybe "restaurant" is a bit generous. These pizza emporiums are something else. The food is adequate, but the experience is, well, something kids go nuts over.

Experience may well be the highest level of economic value. In our prosperous world of the early twenty-first century, consumers in developed countries have most of the tangible goods they need. Those fortunate enough to benefit from the recent economy have about all the luxury cars, quality clothes, and trendy coffees they can handle. People today are using more expendable income to enjoy experiences such as entertainment, travel, cruises, spas, and retreat centers.

Smart companies are making their customers' contact with it an experience. An experience occurs when the company's core products are used as props to engage individual customers in a way that creates a memorable event.[8]

Examples of events include live entertainment at restaurants and coffee shop chats at bookstores. Sporting events and competitions may place the company's products in the background, but the customer receives value from the event itself because ties to the company are likely to follow.

//

Companies can provide A-plus value by making customer transactions memorable experiences.

//

When A-plussing value with customer experiences, it is important not to forget the core product. Planet Hollywood was a hot company in the mid-1990s only to crash when people realized that the glitzy experience of perhaps seeing a celebrity was not worth eating the substandard food.

Experiences can enhance the sense of value as long as the core product remains of good quality.

Build A-Plus Value with Uniqueness and Shared Values

An enhanced sense of value can stem from being perceived as unique or novel. Much of this uniqueness arises from the personality or culture of your organization. Ben and Jerry's ice cream business projects a sense of culture based on the liberal political values of its founders and its sense of civic responsibility to Vermont. (The ice cream plant tours are the most popular tourist attraction in the state.) Their theme has been consistent throughout the history of the company and has been the subject of books, articles, and television magazine shows.

Southwest Airlines (SWA) does a good job of conveying a charming quirkiness that reflects its CEO, Herb Kelleher. The airline started as a scrappy little outfit and has grown into an aviation powerhouse, in part because its customers like the people who work there. SWA hires people based on their attitudes, not necessarily skills. New skills can be taught; attitudes seldom change much.

The interview process and new employee orientation are uniquely tailored to help people fit the corporate culture. For example, new employees engage in a scavenger hunt to find answers to company orientation questions.

Customers often go out of their way to support companies that share their values. Talk show host Rush Limbaugh and news commentator Paul

Harvey have been credited with launching many popular brands because listeners who share their views feel they are getting enhanced value from companies that agree with them.

Political, church, civic, alumni, and charitable groups often band together to promote or support certain organizations. The results of this bonding may range from affinity credit cards to cell phones decorated with a hockey team logo to the purchase of Girl Scout cookies. In the end, the customer comes away with an enhanced sense of value.

///
Customers experience enhanced value in products that support their interests, causes, or affiliations.
///

On a more local basis, we become loyal to companies that make us feel comfortable. We patronize organizations that reflect our values and preferences.

Build A-Plus Value with Credibility

Customers also feel they are receiving extra value when dealing with companies that have exceptional credibility. A critical dimension of value is the degree to which your customers trust you. Failure to follow through on commitments and other deceptive practices can, and should, destroy a company. Of course, sometimes this, too, is perceptual. You feel you explained a policy or guarantee to your customers and they interpret it differently. You think you communicated openly and the customer sees your limitations as unnecessary "fine print" nitpicking.

Keep Promises Simple and Understandable

Give A-plus value by keeping things simple and understandable for customers. The competing long-distance telephone companies have made some strides to simplify their calling plans. Most now offer one rate for calls at any time during the day with no hidden charges. It took them a while to get there, but now at least the customer understands and can make a rational choice without fearing deceptive practices.

The airlines, on the other hand, do a poor job of building credibility with customers and will, I predict, one day pay a price for their evasiveness, their "fine print" sleight of hand, and their enormous fare discrepancies. Indeed, customer complaints against airlines are growing at a rate nearly eight times that of passengers, according to the industry's own figures.[9] Complaints about the airline industry skyrocketed in 2000 even as air carriers promised to treat customers better "and be more forthright with passengers all the way through their travel experience." When Transportation Department inspectors checked to find out whether the airlines were living up to that pledge, they found varying degrees of success.[10]

On any given flight you will find passengers who have paid up to ten times as much as another passenger for the same service: transportation from point A to point B. You may be delighted with your $200 fare while the guy next to you paid $1,000 or more, depending on when the ticket was booked and many other factors. In short, the airlines' fare systems are unintelligible to their customers, creating a lack of trust.

Avoid Frequent Flyer–Type Fiascoes

Frequent flyer programs are similarly confusing and often perceived as untrustworthy. While frequent flyer miles entice passengers to fly the same airline, the promised rewards come only with a lot of strings attached. Customers who accumulate miles too often find that the promised free tickets or service-class upgrades are simply not available. What the airlines do not freely tell us is that each flight has only a few "award travel" seats. They also don't mention blackout dates, upgrades that cannot be offered from a certain class of ticket, and other limitations. In short, they shoot their corporate credibility in the foot with lavish promises that too often are not delivered. In fact, seats available for reward travel range from as low as 4.9 percent to 9.8 percent. The average is about 6 percent—six seats out of a hundred.[11] I personally tried to redeem a Delta Airlines frequent flyer seat by booking four months in advance and was told the flight was sold out.

Airlines insist that they are not trying to make it hard to redeem miles for tickets. The problem, they say, is that with planes carrying record numbers of passengers, the demand for free seats far exceeds the space available.

//

You can't A-plus value when your customers don't trust you.

//

Follow Up on Commitments Made

Another common credibility destroyer is failure to follow up on commitments. I recently purchased a rather pricey used car from the Utah Auto Collection, an organization touted as a no-dicker, full-service auto consortium created by Ford. Among the many frustrations experienced, I was given just one key to the car and promised that the dealer would get me another because it had lost the backup. After repeated phone calls, I finally gave up, took the car to another dealership, and bought the key—along with several other missing parts, including the CD changer cartridge and all owner's manuals. This was a six-month-old car, by the way. And this was the quality of service I was given after paying $34,000 for the car. The dealership made no effort to get any of these items for me.

The aggravation of getting anything out of the Utah Auto Collection became more than I could handle. I am sure this dealership thinks it won. I quit pestering the staff and they didn't have to buy anything for me. But the price they pay in damaged credibility is showing up. I take every opportunity to tell other people (including students in my large university classes) about this poor value experience.

A newspaper report in the business pages mentioned that this consortium of no-dicker, one-price dealerships was not doing as well as Ford had expected. The article implied that the pricing plan wasn't seen as such a good deal and that customers were not getting as good a price as they expected. A few days later, a letter to the editor contradicted the write-up and lashed into Utah Auto Collection, saying that price has nothing to do with this company's disappointing results. The writer had received similarly poor service and misleading, unresponsive attitudes and was sharing his experience with others.

There can be no A-plus value without credibility. The solutions to the kinds of problems described here are either to not offer incentives you cannot provide or to make good on your word. Those are the only choices.

Build A-Plus Value with Add-Ons

One of the simplest ways to surprise customers is to give them something unexpected—or sell them something else they may need. When a shoe store clerk gives a shoehorn with a pair of new shoes or asks if you'd like to try padded inserts or a pair of lifetime-guarantee socks, the salesperson is using the A-plus value approach. Sometimes add-ons are sold, sometimes given away. Both can be effective. A clerk at a supermarket hands customers a few candy kisses with the receipt, an unexpected thank you. The hotel check-in desk has a basket of complimentary apples or a plate of fresh-baked cookies. The paint store salesperson checks to be sure buyers have caulking and sandpaper.

The best kinds of free add-ons are those with high perceived value and low cost to the business. For example, gas stations that give away a free car wash with fill-up are offering something that costs them a few cents (water and soap—not counting, of course, the cost of the equipment), but their customers receive a service with a perceived value of $3 to $4 (which is the price printed on the coupon). Free popcorn or drinks given away with video rentals cost three or four cents, but have a much higher perceived value (really high, when compared to the price of movie theater popcorn!).

//
Give away something of perceived value and you tip the equity scale in your favor.
//

Obviously, this A-plus opportunity area ties in closely with its marketing counterpart, add-on sales. Marketers have long recognized the value of trying to sell current customers something else as long as you have them there. This practice can backfire if it's too pushy, but most customers will not resent low-key inquiries about other products. The hardware salesperson who checks with the customer to be sure he has the right tools is not going to be resented. And the company may well sell some additional products.

One of the more creative add-ons came out of a seminar I ran a few years ago. A woman attending the session owned several quick-lube shops. When we talked about add-ons she came up with this idea: When people bought a full-service oil change, she did what her competitors have been doing. She checked all fluids, washed windows, checked tire pressure, and vacuumed the car's interior. But then she had this add-on idea. She ran a cassette head cleaning tape through the customer's sound system. Now we all know that cleaning the cassette tape player this way makes for better sound, but most people never get around to it. After running the cleaning tape, she inserted a preprinted card into the tape player noting that the heads had been cleaned courtesy of her company. It cost her practically nothing, but provided a clear and distinctive add-on for her customers.

//
Add-ons can be a simple and enjoyable way to surprise your customers.
//

Central to the philosophy of add-ons is the belief that you cannot give away more than you eventually receive. That is a tough concept for many people to accept. But, at some philosophical level, you need to be comfortable with the belief that what goes around comes around. In fact, that is fundamental to all the A-plus loyalty-building strategies. You really will benefit from generosity. Take the leap of faith and reap the rewards of greater customer loyalty.

SELF-EVALUATION: HOW ARE YOU BUILDING A-PLUS VALUE?

How well are you creating an enhanced sense of value? Circle yes or no for each of the following statements. Then consider which of these ideas could be immediately implemented to build A-plus value.

My company (department, store, or organization):

1. Regularly considers possible packaging options that could enhance the sense of value.   Yes   No
   What we could do: _____
2. Reviews our warranty or guarantee policies to provide the most liberal possible protection for our customers.   Yes   No
   What we could do: _____

3. Is aware of and implementing the most sophisticated customer contact management systems appropriate for our business. Yes   No
   What we could do: _____

4. Carefully considers goodness of fit and personalization of our products and services for the maximum benefit of our customers. Yes   No
   What we could do: _____

5. Uses "experiences" to attract and satisfy customers.   Yes   No
   What we could do: _____

6. Positions itself as consistent with our customers' values. We understand the kinds of values our customers adhere to and show them how our products coincide with those values.   Yes   No
   What we could do: _____

7. Constantly strives to be totally trustworthy and to build impeccable credibility in all we do.   Yes   No
   What we could do: _____

8. Offers customer pricing, incentive programs, and policies that are forthright and simple to understand.   Yes   No
   What we could do: _____

WORKSHEETS:
GIVING CUSTOMERS A-PLUS VALUE

🖎 PACKAGING IDEAS

Use this form to brainstorm possible A-plus packaging ideas. Working alone or with a small group, jot down as many ideas as possible without regard for whether they are practical or immediately usable. Then review all ideas for possible adoption by your organization. Put a checkmark next to the ones you want to try.

☐
☐
☐
☐
☐

Develop a priority list indicating when you will apply each selected idea. Describe tasks or resources necessary to enact the A-plus ideas.

A-plus Packaging Priorities	*Implementation Requirements*
1.	Time Frame:
	Tasks:
	Task Responsibility:
2.	Time Frame:
	Tasks:
	Task Responsibility:
3.	Time Frame:
	Tasks:
	Task Responsibility:

✍ GUARANTEE AND WARRANTY IDEAS

Use this form to brainstorm possible A-plus ideas about guarantees and warranties. Working alone or with a small group, jot down as many ideas as possible without regard for whether they are practical or immediately usable. Then review all ideas for possible adoption by your organization. Put a checkmark next to the ones you want to try.

☐
☐
☐
☐
☐

Develop a priority list indicating when you will apply each selected idea. Describe tasks or resources necessary to enact the A-plus ideas.

Guarantee/Warranty
Priorities   *Implementation Requirements*

                                    Time Frame:
1.
                                    Tasks:

                                    Task Responsibility:

2.   Time Frame:

                                    Tasks:

                                    Task Responsibility:

3.   Time Frame:

                                    Tasks:

                                    Task Responsibility:

☜ GOODNESS-OF-FIT IDEAS

Use this form to brainstorm possible A-plus ideas for improving goodness of fit between your products and customer needs. Working alone or with a small group, jot down as many ideas as possible without regard for whether they are practical or immediately usable. Then review all ideas for possible adoption by your organization. Put a checkmark next to the ones you want to try.

☐

☐

☐

☐

☐

Develop a priority list indicating when you will apply each selected idea. Describe tasks or resources necessary to enact the A-plus ideas.

Goodness-of-Fit Priorities	*Implementation Requirements*
1.	Time Frame:
	Tasks:
	Task Responsibility:
2.	Time Frame:
	Tasks:
	Task Responsibility:
3.	Time Frame:
	Tasks:
	Task Responsibility:

▱ MEMORABLE EXPERIENCES IDEAS

Use this form to brainstorm possible A-plus ideas for making customer experiences with you more memorable. Working alone or with a small group, jot down as many ideas as possible without regard for whether they are practical or immediately usable. Then review all ideas for possible adoption by your organization. Put a checkmark next to the ones you want to try.

☐
☐
☐
☐
☐

Develop a priority list indicating when you will apply each selected idea. Describe tasks or resources necessary to enact the A-plus ideas.

Top Ideas for Creating Memorable Experiences	*Implementation Requirements*
1.	Time Frame:
	Tasks:
	Task Responsibility:
2.	Time Frame:
	Tasks:
	Task Responsibility:
3.	Time Frame:
	Tasks:
	Task Responsibility:

✍ UNIQUE AND SHARED VALUES IDEAS

Use this form to brainstorm possible A-plus ideas for demonstrating to customers your shared values . Working alone or with a small group, jot down as many ideas as possible without regard for whether they are practical or immediately usable. Then review all ideas for possible adoption by your organization. Put a checkmark next to the ones you want to try.

☐
☐
☐
☐
☐

Develop a priority list indicating when you will apply each selected idea. Describe tasks or resources necessary to enact the A-plus ideas.

Top Unique/Shared Values Ideas

Implementation Requirements

1.   Time Frame:

   Tasks:

   Task Responsibility:

2.   Time Frame:

   Tasks:

   Task Responsibility:

3.   Time Frame:

   Tasks:

   Task Responsibility:

CREDIBILITY ENHANCEMENT IDEAS

Use this form to brainstorm possible A-plus ideas for projecting enhanced credibility. Working alone or with a small group, jot down as many ideas as possible without regard for whether they are practical or immediately usable. Then review all ideas for possible adoption by your organization. Put a checkmark next to the ones you want to try.

☐

☐

☐

☐

☐

Develop a priority list indicating when you will apply each selected idea. Describe tasks or resources necessary to enact the A-plus ideas.

Top Credibility Enhancers	*Implementation Requirements*
1.	Time Frame:
	Tasks:
	Task Responsibility:
2.	Time Frame:
	Tasks:
	Task Responsibility:
3.	Time Frame:
	Tasks:
	Task Responsibility:

◢ ADD-ON IDEAS

Use this form to brainstorm possible A-plus value ideas using add-ons. What kinds of things can you give away (or sell) to make your core products more valuable to customers? Working alone or with a small group, jot down as many ideas as possible without regard for whether they are practical or immediately usable. Then review all ideas for possible adoption by your organization. Put a checkmark next to the ones you want to try.

☐
☐
☐
☐
☐

Develop a priority list indicating when you will apply each selected idea. Describe tasks or resources necessary to enact the A-plus ideas.

Add-On Priorities	*Implementation Requirements*
1.	Time Frame:
	Tasks:
	Task Responsibility:
2.	Time Frame:
	Tasks:
	Task Responsibility:
3.	Time Frame:
	Tasks:
	Task Responsibility:

Notes

1. B. Joseph Pine II, and James H. Gilmore, "Welcome to the Experience Economy," *Harvard Business Review* (July–August 1998), p. 97.
2. Michael Schuman and Hae Won Choi, "Suwon's Restrooms, Once the Pits, Are Flush with Tourists," *The Wall Street Journal* (November 26, 1999), p. A1.
3. Toyota once ran a series of TV commercials that depicted a driver stepping out of a ten-year-old model perched on top of a mountain. The actor looks into the camera and announces that he has over 300,000 miles on his truck. Although the spot never featured the new truck model, the implication was there: Buy a new truck and it'll exceed your expectations for long-term value.
4. "Lands' End Guarantee Verboten in Germany," *The* (Salt Lake City) *Deseret News* (AP), (September 25, 1999), p. B-1.
5. Interview with Randall Myers, senior knowledge engineer, Sterling Wentworth Corporation, Salt Lake City, October 1999.
6. Brittany Martin, in "Letters to Fortune," *Fortune* (January 12, 1998), p. 19.
7. "Mass Customization Becomes the New Marketing Mantra," *The Wall Street Journal* (April 29, 1999), p. A1.
8. Pine and Gilmore, p. 98.
9. Clifton Leaf, "The Death of Customer Service," *Smart Money* (October 1998), pp. 131–137.
10. Jesse J. Holland, "Complaints against Airline Industry on the Rise, Report Finds," Nando Media, copyright AP, June 28, 2000.
11. Melynda Dovel Wilcox and Lynn Woods, "Desperately Seeking Seats," *Kiplinger's Personal Finance Magazine* (July 1999), pp. 88–92.

Chapter 6

Strategy 5: Give Customers A-Plus Information

Every product has an informational component, and with that comes an A-plus opportunity.

The Way It Is . . .

I n 1987 I bought an Acura Legend automobile. At that time, Acura was a brand-new product line produced by Honda's luxury division. Honda chose to set up an entirely separate network of dealers to sell the Acura line. When I bought my car, I was introduced to A-plus information.

Based on my purchasing experience with dozens of cars, I anticipated that the salesperson would tell me to read the owner's manual in the glove box to figure out how to use the various accessories and features of the car. Instead, the sales representative spent about thirty minutes with me—after the sale—showing me how to program the radio, where to check and add oil, how to find and use the jack, spare tire, and tool kit. He even showed me how to maintain the car's finish. In short, he gave me the detailed instruction I needed to make the most of my purchase. This far exceeded any previous experience with auto dealerships.

Another A-plus information experience happened a few years ago when my teenage son had knee surgery. After the surgery he was referred to a physical therapist. I anticipated that the therapist would show him how to exercise the knees to aid in recovery. She did this, but also added some small touches I saw as A-plus. She photocopied pictures of each exercise, wrote his name on the pages in large red letters, taught him each exercise, gave him her home phone number, and encouraged him to call with any questions. She even called him the next day to see how he was doing. Little things? Sure they were. But the composite of these little things went beyond what we had anticipated and created an A-plus experience.

The dot-com e-tailers are learning about the importance of A-plus information, with some of these businesses doing better than others. A friend's recent online purchase through MotherNature.com resulted in a less satisfactory exchange of information. MotherNature.com sent a message saying the order would be shipped within three to four days, but the order did not arrive as promised. When the customer inquired about when she could expect the merchandise ordered, she was again told inaccurate information—information that promised a shipment that did not arrive. A few days later, the customer found the product she ordered, which was valued at several hundred dollars, on her doorstep, having been left out in the rain all night. All this because the company failed to give correct and timely information.

My recent experience with VitaminShoppe.com also failed badly in the information area. While the web page touted special next-day-delivery service at no extra charge, in reality, the merchandise I ordered on Monday still had not arrived on Friday. My e-mail to the company was unanswered. I finally called and was told that part of my order had been shipped and the back-ordered portion would be shipped in two days. A day later I received the following e-mail message (reprinted exactly as I received it):

Dear Valued Customer,
The following item(s) within your order #WO3690775 have been updated, and now have the following status:

SKU # IN-2027	-Processing;
SKU # TQ-1010	-Shipped;
SKU # VS-1135	-Shipped;
SKU # UE-1003	-Shipped;

Does this information make any sense to you? It sure didn't to me. The company's message was filled with internal jargon that means nothing to the customer. Customers don't refer to products ordered by SKU numbers, and the status report of "processing" tells nothing. The opportunity to A-plus customers with useful information is obviously a foreign concept to this company. For that matter, communicating with any clarity also seems unimportant to the company, based on my firsthand experience.

Some e-tailers acknowledge orders more clearly, but provide incomplete information. Customers sometimes receive order confirmations that fail to describe what was ordered (just as the above-mentioned order status report did), the exact delivery date, or the cost. Such incomplete information does little good for people who use the Net for frequent shopping.

In fairness, some e-tailers are getting it right. Online florist Proflowers.com, for example, tells the customer when the ordered flowers were picked up from the distributor, when they were delivered, and even who accepted the delivery. My experiences with Proflowers have reinforced my loyalty. A Christmas wreath order to my sister in Iowa was scheduled for delivery December 15. Proflowers called me on December 12 and left a voice message, asking me to contact them on their toll-free line about this order. When I called, they apologized for failing to get the order faxed to their Iowa distributor and advised me the shipment would be one day late. They then waived the shipping charge. With practices such as these, Proflowers is creating the standard in the young and quickly evolving online business world. Customers are quickly coming to anticipate e-tailers sending immediate acknowledgments telling the precise status of order, the shipping date, and costs. Companies that fail to meet this level of service will soon be left in the e-business dust.

A-Plus Information: What It Is

Every product, service, or purchasing experience has an informational component. Food items offer nutritional data, preparation tips, and recipes. Automobiles, appliances, and electronic equipment have owner's manuals. Lawn services tell us how to care for the grass. Exercise equipment comes with a range of options for getting the most from the product. People expect to receive such information.

///
Information is needed for people to get the full benefit of virtually all products or services.
///

SELF-EVALUATION: WHAT ARE THE INFORMATIONAL COMPONENTS?

Consider several products or services you have recently purchased. What are the informational components of each? How well does the company meet or exceed your expectations with regard to information? Here is an example:

Product or Service	Information Provided	Adequacy/ Effectiveness of Information	What Else Could the Company Do?
Health club membership	Brochure of services; schedule of classes	Okay but not very imaginative; simple photocopied handouts	Creative booklet with cartoons; videotape introduction to classes

You can create a table with examples based on your own purchasing experiences or, better, based on your organization's product or service offerings. How well does your organization meet or exceed its customers expectations with regard to information?

The Special Demands of E-Commerce

For e-commerce, timely information on the status of customer orders is especially important to retention and loyalty. Online customers may feel left in a vacuum if the company does not communicate efficiently, clearly, and in a timely manner. The online newsletter *Internet Daily* has reported that many online brokerages flunk the service test:

> Online brokerages have a lot of work to do to improve customer service. Researchers at Jupiter Communications tested twenty-five websites' rates of response to customers' messages. Among financial-services sites, 39 percent responded in one day, while the balance took up to three days or, in the case of 25 percent, never responded.[1]

Information handling provides an opportunity for surprising customers. A-plus information happens when customers receive information that's more timely, clearer, or more useful than they anticipated.

///
A-plus information is more timely, clearer, or more useful than the customer anticipates.
///

How to Produce A-Plus Information

Let's look at some specific ways to create an A-plus information experience for customers. This chapter considers informational hand-holding, media selection, message clarity, information accessibility, and user groups to get you thinking about A-plus information ideas.

Provide Informational Hand-Holding

As discussed previously, the explosive growth of electronic commerce provides a golden opportunity to exceed what customers anticipate with A-plus information. The young and rapidly changing e-tailing world offers a wide range of service levels as many companies work to figure out how to do commerce online well. Customers are just beginning to develop loyalties to certain e-tailers and bookmarking select websites on their computers. Until customers feel completely comfortable about the information they receive, they are likely to do as 90 percent of 1999 Christmas shoppers did: Examine merchandise on the Net, then purchase it offline at brick-and-mortar retailers. "Customers say they aren't filling electronic shopping carts because they don't get enough hand-holding on the Net. Indeed, research shows that 90 percent of online customers prefer human interaction."[2]

One reason people are hesitating to use electronic commerce is that they don't feel confident—they need more hand-holding.

Getting useful, reassuring information into the heads of customers should be an important part of the development of any e-commerce efforts. Scripps Howard technology journalist James Derk offers this caution: "Once you venture into online commerce, do it right. If you screw up in your brick-and-mortar store, you may offend one or two people. If you mess up in cyberspace, you can offend thousands, who will tell thousands more that your store is run by incompetent loons."[3]

While web-based companies have a great opportunity to improve the information they give customers, such opportunities are not limited to e-commerce. Every organization can produce A-plus information.

Hand-holding isn't just for electronic businesses. Most companies can do better at reducing customer anxiety and making them feel more at home.

But hand-holding isn't just for electronic commerce. Better organizations of all types are increasingly sensitive to customer discomfort and

ANOTHER LOOK: ONLINE SHOPPING

Online shoppers during Christmas 1999 spent about $8 billion, double what they spent in 1998. But, says a *Forbes* magazine article, "they would be spending billions more if websites were easier to use. Two-thirds of all online shopping carts get abandoned before checkout. . . . Only 2 percent of the people who click to an online store buy anything. Yet back in the real world, more than half of the customers who walk into a shopping mall make a purchase."[4]

are making efforts to reduce it. Companies that have personal guides, personal shoppers, and private bankers are doing hand-holding. Companies that have effective receptionists or greeters who keep customers informed of matters of interest to them are doing hand-holding. Organizational leaders who give customers their home phone numbers and invite them to call if they have problems or concerns are doing hand-holding, too.

Look carefully at your company. Are you providing ways to make customers comfortable and confident as they do business with you?

Select Informational Media Carefully

When providing customers with information, consider various media options. Media should be chosen on the basis of communication effectiveness, not just efficiency. Let me explain.

///
Communication efficiency and effectiveness are not the same.
///

Communication *efficiency* is the simple ratio of the costs of communicating relative to the number of people reached by the message. If a message is extremely simple (e.g., a no-parking sign, a memo announcing a price change on a particular product, a simple cooking tip or recipe), we can get away with an efficient medium such as a flyer, label, or simple instruction sheet. As soon as we go beyond the simplest messages, however, communication effectiveness becomes more important.

Communication *effectiveness* is different from communication efficiency. Effectiveness is achieved when the message is:

→ Received by the right people (and not others)
→ Easily understood
→ Remembered for a reasonable amount of time
→ Applied

The media that best achieve effectiveness are seldom simple or cheap. The greatest effectiveness is typically achieved when people talk face-to-face. This, of course, is much more expensive and far less efficient than an instruction sheet. But if the message is crucial to the customer's satisfaction with the product, it will be well worth the extra cost. My Acura dealer apparently believed in paying the price for personalized, face-to-face communication when he taught me about the features of my new car.

Much misunderstanding can be attributed to overemphasizing efficiency when we should stress effectiveness. Sometimes it doesn't pay to be efficient. The cheap, easy way to give information (e.g., the e-mail from the VitaminShoppe) doesn't do the job.

Creative companies seek to become A-plus by breaking away from the usual, efficient medium and by using a variety of media for various messages. Chevrolet, for example, goes beyond the owner's manual and provides an audiotape to teach customers how to use the features of their car or truck. Some companies provide videotapes to teach customers how to assemble or use a product. Online help and telephone hotlines (if well designed and responsive) have saved many a frustrated consumer.

Continental Cablevision of St. Paul, Minnesota, has gone one better. It programmed a channel called "TV House Call" in which a company representative demonstrates, live, the solution to an individual subscriber's problem while the customer is watching. A company spokesperson says, "People are absolutely astounded. You can almost see jaws dropping at the other end of the phone when they experience this [service]."[5]

Many organizations now have online help services with frequently asked questions (FAQs). The best ones use several levels of FAQs that address the needs of prospects and newer customers with somewhat basic questions, and others for registered customers who know their way around the company's products and services.[6]

Companies can readily anticipate the frequently asked questions and provide answers before these are even asked.

In the early days of personal computers, documentation (i.e., the instruction manual) was notoriously bad. It was hard to read and often grammatically incorrect. Today's computer or software user wouldn't stand for that for a minute. The informational bar has been raised considerably. What passed for the norm in 1980 would be totally unacceptable in today's plug-and-play world.

Progressive companies are constantly looking for media options that allow them to A-plus their customers.

Constantly Strive for Message Clarity

Regardless of the media used, information must be clear and understandable and correct. Companies need to seek clarity by presenting their messages with short, clear sentences, a logical sequence of information, and enough repetition to effectively teach the message receiver.

Consider an Audit of Your Company's Writing

Many organizations could benefit from having a professional business communication expert do an audit of their written documents, telephone scripts, and presentations. My colleague Dr. Sherron Bienvenu of Emory University recently completed a project for an Atlanta company that recognized that its written documents were not of the quality it wanted. Bienvenu analyzed a sample of the letters and memos sent to the client's customers and quickly recognized some patterns that could be improved upon. Among the problems she found are some you, too, may be experiencing in your documents:

1. *Abrupt Tone.* While most readers appreciate business writers getting directly to the point, many of these letters were too abrupt.

2. *Use of Cliches or Jargon.* Cliches are overused, stale phrases; jargon is specialized language the company may well understand but the customer may not. If you are not sure the customer will know the meaning of a term (e.g., SKU numbers in my earlier example), use a simpler, clearer description.

3. *Use of Stock Numbers or Abbreviations.* The reader may not understand or recognize this information.

4. *Failure to Express Appreciation.* The most powerful phrase in any relationship is probably "thank you." Instead of telling a customer that her order cannot be shipped as planned, start the message with a "thank you for ordering" or "thank you for your patience."

5. *Failure to Offer an Alternative to Solve a Problem.* Don't just tell a customer reading your literature what you cannot do; tell her what you can do.

6. *Failure to Provide a Reasonable Explanation.* Don't say "it's against our policy" and think that's a sufficient statement. Take a moment to explain why the policy is as it is.

//
Some common problems can arise in business writing that obscure rather than clarify.
//

As any author would testify, we can constantly improve the wording of almost anything we write or say. Being willing to edit and reedit messages is critical to ongoing improvement and provides the opportunity to create A-plus information.

Use Some Redundancy

Some redundancy in information is often needed to ensure that a message is clearly communicated. People don't always get your messages immediately. For example, you get better results by presenting information verbally (with words) and graphically (with pictures or diagrams). Likewise, an owner's manual with a supplemental video, reference chart, online help program, or 800 hotline can improve the likelihood of customer satisfaction with your product. Such redundant systems are keys to making sure all your customers develop an understanding of your message.

//
Some repetition is almost always needed to get a message across effectively; consider using several media to produce useful redundancy.
//

Make Key Information Easily Accessible with Graphics and Icons

Sometime A-plus information can be as simple as providing clear signs. I consulted with a hospital that had a rather unusual floor plan. What appeared to be the main entrance opened onto a large foyer area with a reception desk. Because the local folks knew that just about everyone came in through the emergency room entryway, this reception area was not staffed. People unfamiliar with the hospital would come in this front door and have no idea where to go. We improved the signs and added some color-coded strips on the floor to lead to various departments.

///
Something as simple as clear signs can help make an A-plus experience for your customers.
///

Signage can also have other benefits. One example comes from Wal-Mart pharmacies. Pharmacy employees faced the large burden of stocking all those little bottles, jars, and boxes in perfectly straight rows in aisle after aisle. Every time a customer picked something up to read the label, the display needed to be straightened or the products turned to face front. It was a lot of work. Wal-Mart tried an experiment: It began replacing traditional shelves with a system of bins. Instead of facing a shelf of aspirin bottles, say, the shopper saw a blowup of the aspirin bottle's label. Under that blowup was the bin, into which the aspirin bottles had been dumped.

The enlarged sign provided A-plus information and solved the time-consuming problem of stocking the shelves—a clerk could just roll a trolley of merchandise to the aisle, open the bin, dump in the goods, and move on. No more arranging products in straight lines.

Shoppers liked it better, too—instead of facing a row of bottles with tiny print, they saw a large, easy-to-read version of the label. It was much easier on the eyes, especially for elderly shoppers.

Create and Support Customer User Groups and Classes

Organizations that bring groups of customers together to form user groups are also offering A-plus information. User groups are naturals for craft shops, computer stores, and financial institutions, and may also work in other arenas. Food stores can offer cooking classes. Credit unions can sponsor complimentary classes on investments, budgeting, and personal finance. Auto repair shops can offer classes on auto maintenance.

One of my clients was a medium-size tire shop and auto repair business. While brainstorming ideas for giving A-plus information, the employees decided to offer auto maintenance classes, specifically aimed at their female customers. Through some creative advertising and frequent mention of the classes to customers, they got a pretty good turnout. The classes covered tips for tire care, guided tours of a car's exhaust system (with a mechanic showing the parts of a car on a lift), even a session on maintaining auto paint and upholstery. The groups were small at first, then grew as customers became aware that the classes ran every Tuesday evening at seven o'clock. And you can bet those who attended the classes were loyal customers.

///
Free classes for product customers or potential customers can create A-plus information.
///

Businesses should try to increase the level of interaction with their customers, using any available media. If a business values its customers as its principal asset, it will want to interact with those customers at every conceivable opportunity. Such interactivity can occur in a wide variety of ways.

A-Plus Information in E-Commerce

As discussed previously, e-commerce faces some special challenges and opportunities in providing A-plus information. Two critical actions are to make customer support easily accessible and to honor the customer feedback loop.

Make Customer Support Accessible

One of the greatest challenges of business today is providing timely, effective support to customers who have questions. E-commerce is especially vulnerable to complaints of lack of support. Electronic commerce relies heavily (sometimes too heavily) on e-mail for communicating with customers.

Julie Schoenfeld, president of Net Effect, a California-based website developer, describes a commonly heard complaint about e-commerce: "That companies by design are leaving their phone numbers off [their

websites] because they don't want to spend money on having someone
stand by and answer the phone. . . . Their feeling is, 'We ought to be able
to answer questions on the Web.' " Indeed, surveys show that 40 percent
of companies don't provide an e-mail address for customers to ask questions, and 75 percent don't post phone numbers.[7]

//
ANOTHER LOOK: HANDLING MASSIVE REQUEST VOLUME WITH GOOD FAQs

Can ten employees cover 550,000 customers? An article in *Smart
Business* asked this question and illustrated how even a relatively small
staff can handle huge customer volume. WebJump.com hosts a free
website for its half million customers. Without a staff or the budget to
hire a SWAT team of people to take customer support calls, WebJump
developed a dynamic FAQs service to handle the vast majority of customer questions. A company executive estimates it would cost $40
million a year to provide the same service via telephone or e-mail.[8]
//

Honor the Customer Feedback Loop

A related and all-too-common complaint of e-tail buyers is the lack of
responsiveness when customers do contact the company with a problem.
A survey by the e-tailer trade group Shop.org showed that about a quarter
of shoppers never received a response to an e-mail request for assistance.
"It's Retailing 101: Don't ignore your customers," says Mary Helen Gil-
lespie, president of E-BuyersGuide.com. "Plus, it's not just bad business,
it's extremely rude even by today's standards."[9]

//
Ignoring customer requests is just plain rude.
//

Making your company more accessible to your customers is an excellent
way to exceed customer expectations and surprise them with service that's
better than anticipated. But if you offer help lines, be sure they are adequately staffed with knowledgeable people who can honor customer requests for information with a timely response.

How to Measure Your A-Plus Information Efforts

Log Common Questions (FAQs)

Develop a system for keeping track of common customer questions. If several people are asking the same questions or experiencing similar confusion, you have an information problem. This advice applies to all companies, not just the technologically sophisticated. The smallest shop can make note of recurring customer concerns.

To develop a system for gathering such information, you need to make it worthwhile for employees to record and pass on the customer's feedback. Offer employees incentives for listing and reporting customer comments. Invite customers to tell you what they are thinking either in writing or orally. (Writing inhibits many comments because it is troublesome for many people to take the time to write. Therefore, teach your employees to make notes of customer responses, preferably in front of customers so that they know they are being heard.)

Audit Your Company's Communication

A communication audit is a process for determining the quantity and quality of information flowing through the company as well as that coming into the organization from outside stakeholders. Many auditing techniques are used to assess the communicative health of a company. In most cases it makes sense to hire a communication consultant to do the audit. An effective consultant will be able to maintain objectivity, pinpoint communication roadblocks, identify overload problems, and assess the effectiveness of the company's formal and informal communication networks. However, the next section outlines a process you can use to do an initial customer communication audit.

Self-Evaluation: A Customer Communication Audit

Customize the instrument presented here to invite your customers to describe the amount of information they currently receive from your company compared with the amount of information they feel they need to receive to make a more informed decision about your products or services. This exercise can assess current efforts and suggest approaches for improvement.

Use the following five-point scale, ask your customers to circle the number that best describes the quantity of information provided to them:

1 = Very little   4 = A lot
2 = Little   5 = A great amount
3 = Some   n/a = Not applicable

Type of Information	What I Receive Now	What I Need to Receive
Face-to-face contact with one employee (one-to-one service)	1 2 3 4 5 n/a	1 2 3 4 5 n/a
Face-to-face contact among more than two people (group support)	1 2 3 4 5 n/a	1 2 3 4 5 n/a
Telephone support	1 2 3 4 5 n/a	1 2 3 4 5 n/a
Product documentation, owner's guides, instructions for assembly and use, etc.	1 2 3 4 5 n/a	1 2 3 4 5 n/a
Videos, audiotapes, electronic media	1 2 3 4 5 n/a	1 2 3 4 5 n/a
Online help; web page guidance	1 2 3 4 5 n/a	1 2 3 4 5 n/a
Written newsletters, information bulletins, fact sheets	1 2 3 4 5 n/a	1 2 3 4 5 n/a
Other communications (please specify)	1 2 3 4 5 n/a	1 2 3 4 5 n/a

WORKSHEETS:
GIVING CUSTOMERS A-PLUS INFORMATION

✍ HAND-HOLDING IDEAS

Use this form to brainstorm possible A-plus information ideas. How can your organization better provide customer hand-holding? Working alone or with a small group, jot down as many ideas as possible without regard for whether they are practical or immediately usable. Then review all ideas for possible adoption by your organization. Put a checkmark next to the ones you want to try.

☐

☐

☐

☐

☐

Develop a priority list indicating when you will apply each selected idea. Describe tasks or resources necessary to enact the A-plus ideas.

Best Hand-Holding Ideas	*Implementation Requirements*
1.	Time Frame:
	Tasks:
	Task Responsibility:
2.	Time Frame:
	Tasks:
	Task Responsibility:
3.	Time Frame:
	Tasks:
	Task Responsibility:

◢ MEDIA USE IDEAS

Use this form to brainstorm possible A-plus information ideas. How can your organization better use various communication media to provide better customer information? Working alone or with a small group, jot down as many ideas as possible without regard for whether they are practical or immediately usable. Then review all ideas for possible adoption by your organization. Put a checkmark next to the ones you want to try.

☐
☐
☐
☐
☐

Develop a priority list indicating when you will apply each selected idea. Describe tasks or resources necessary to enact the A-plus ideas.

Media Use Ideas	*Implementation Requirements*
1.	Time Frame:
	Tasks:
	Task Responsibility:
2.	Time Frame:
	Tasks:
	Task Responsibility:
3.	Time Frame:
	Tasks:
	Task Responsibility:

✍ MESSAGE CLARITY IDEAS

Use this form to brainstorm possible A-plus information ideas. How can your organization improve message clarity on materials you are currently using to provide better customer information? Consider the use of different layouts, icons, or graphics, as well as improved wording. Working alone or with a small group, jot down as many ideas as possible without regard for whether they are practical or immediately usable. Then review all ideas for possible adoption by your organization. Put a checkmark next to the ones you want to try.

☐
☐
☐
☐
☐

Develop a priority list indicating when you will apply each selected idea. Describe tasks or resources necessary to enact the A-plus ideas.

Ideas for Making Messages
Clearer   *Implementation Requirements*

1.   Time Frame:

                                       Tasks:

                                       Task Responsibility:

2.   Time Frame:

                                       Tasks:

                                       Task Responsibility:

3.   Time Frame:

                                       Tasks:

                                       Task Responsibility:

✍ USER GROUPS OR CLASSES IDEAS

Use this form to brainstorm possible A-plus information ideas. How might your organization initiate user groups or classes to provide customers with better information? Working alone or with a small group, jot down as many ideas as possible without regard for whether they are practical or immediately usable. Then review all ideas for possible adoption by your organization. Put a checkmark next to the ones you want to try.

☐
☐
☐
☐
☐

Develop a priority list indicating when you will apply each selected idea. Describe tasks or resources necessary to enact the A-plus ideas.

Ideas for Implementing User Groups and Classes	*Implementation Requirements*
1.	Time Frame:
	Tasks:
	Task Responsibility:
2.	Time Frame:
	Tasks:
	Task Responsibility:
3.	Time Frame:
	Tasks:
	Task Responsibility:

Notes

1. Frank Barnako, "Online Brokerages Flunk Service Test," *Internet Daily*, sponsored by CBS MarketWatch, (September 1, 1999).
2. Bill Meyers, "Service with an e-smile," *USA Today* (October 12, 1999), p. B-1.
3. James Derk, "E-Commerce Isn't What It's All Cracked Up to Be," *The* (Salt Lake City) *Deseret News* (November 28, 1999), p. B-3.
4. Silvia Sansoni, "Santa Flaws," *Forbes* (December 27, 1999), p. 282.
5. S. Applebaum, "The Solution Channel," *Cablevision* (July 29, 1992), p. 26.
6. Jim Sterne, *Customer Service on the Internet* (New York: John Wiley & Sons, 1996), p. 26.
7. Pete Barlas, "Buckle Your Seatbelts, It's a Bumpy Ride," *Investor's Business Daily* (September 15, 1999), p. A4.
8. Bonny L. George, "Case Study: Self-Service Support," *Smart Business,* January 2000 (see online edition at www.zdnet.com/smartbusinessmag/ stories).
9. Quoted in Frank Barnako, *Internet Daily*, an online column sponsored by CBS MarketWatch, (September 10, 1999).

Chapter 7

Strategy 6: Show Customers A-Plus Personality

If you want a good indication of the quality of your people management, ask your customers how they are being treated by your employees.

—Ken Blanchard

The Way It Is . . .

Humorist Dave Barry tells this story:

Joe [my attorney] has a client whom I'll call Charles, a mild-mannered financial officer who has never been in any kind of trouble. One evening Charles was driving home from work on the New England Thruway and came to a toll plaza. When his turn came, he pulled up to the booth and held out his $1.25. At this point, the toll-taker pulled out what Charles described as "the biggest pile of one-dollar bills I have ever seen," and started slowly counting them. A minute went by. A line of cars formed behind Charles. Another minute went by. The toll-taker kept counting. Some people behind Charles started honking. *Another* minute went by. Charles sat there, looking in disbelief at the toll-taker, who apparently planned to continue counting the entire pile of bills, and then, who knows, maybe read *War and Peace*. In the lengthening line behind Charles, more people were honking, shouting, gesturing, possibly rummaging through their glove compartments for firearms.

Finally Charles, despite being mild-mannered, did a bad thing. In fact he did *three* bad things: 1) He made an explicit, non-toll-related suggestion to the toll-taker; 2) he threw his $1.25 into the booth; and 3) he drove away.

He did not get far, of course. Western Civilization did not get where it is today by tolerating this kind of flagrant disregard of toll procedures. Charles was swiftly apprehended by two police cars, which escorted him to the police station, where he called Joe, who managed to keep him out of prison through the shrewd legal maneuver of telling him to pay the $50 fine.[1]

Barry's outrageous humor, although exaggerated, makes a point about customer service. It describes the kinds of things that happen when employees either 1) hate their jobs and couldn't care less about customers or 2) are completely ignorant of how certain behaviors come across to others. Let's give this toll-taker the benefit of the doubt and assume that he was simply unaware of how his behavior was being interpreted. That's a stretch, I know, but ignorance is pretty commonplace. Undoubtedly, part of the toll-taker's job was to count the money. That may be a very important part of the job, but his timing was absurd. The ramifications of his actions on others were apparently not within his range of awareness.

A-Plus Personality: What It Is

Customers do business where they enjoy the people. Other things being equal, personal rapport can go a long way toward building customer loyalty. A-plus service exceeds what customers anticipate by presenting a more caring, pleasant, competent, friendly, and comfortable personality.

I recently had lunch at Chicago's O'Hare Airport. What would you anticipate from a busy airport restaurant in a large city? Many people do not associate friendliness with such locations, but I received an excellent service experience. At Wolfgang Puck's restaurant in the terminal I encountered one of the most pleasant, efficient servers. Her name is Ana, and she approached me with the most pleasant smile and friendly chat. She recommended an item on the menu, served me promptly, checked back to see if I needed anything else, refilled my soft drink without waiting for me to ask, and personally wrapped the half of the huge sandwich that I couldn't eat for me to take home. Perhaps the most striking feature of this experience was her radiant smile (I really felt that she enjoyed her work and the customers) and her friendliness. She personified personality and far exceeded what I anticipated from an airport restaurant in a big city.

Human Communication Principles Affecting Personality

Some employees are unaware of the myriad of small and often subtle communication cues that project a positive personality and create A-plus experiences for customers. Personality is a powerful communication tool. Awareness of three principles of human communication can help us better understand how this works.

Communication Principle 1: Anything Can (and Will) Convey a Message

Behaviors convey messages to others via both verbal and nonverbal cues. Our friend the toll-taker used no words but still communicated loud and clear several messages, all of which said he didn't care about his customer. My restaurant server conveyed powerful messages with her smile and pleasant conversation.

We all occasionally communicate the "wrong" message with our nonverbal behaviors. A salesperson who fails to greet a customer, a fellow worker who shows up late, a repair person who leaves a mess, an employee who looks sloppy or dirty—all are communicating something, and usually it is the wrong kind of message.

We constantly send off nonverbal messages to other people that say something about our personality.

Communication Principle 2: The Receiver of the Message Determines What It Means

Everyone thinks they communicate just fine, but ultimately that judgment lies with the message receivers who decide what messages mean. Good intentions, or "what I really meant . . . ," don't matter.

Because our communication style is such a deeply personal thing, changes can be difficult. We communicate the way we do because it seems to work for us. But the best communicators are those who carefully consider the responses of others and consistently make adjustments based on those responses.

Communication Principle 3: Personality Is a Composite of All Communication Behaviors

The conclusions people draw about personalities come from the conclusions drawn from a composite of all communication behaviors. Organizational personality is a composite of the personalities of the employees that customers come in contact with. To project a favorable personality, employees and companies need to be cognizant of the kinds of cues people are paying attention to. And then they need to work toward projecting the most positive messages.

//
An organization's personality is a composite of communicated behaviors perceived by their customers.
//

The remainder of this chapter looks at some of the kinds of behaviors that communicate meaning to customers. This is by no means an exhaustive list of behaviors, but it does reflect the more common ones associated with building customer loyalty.

How to Project A-Plus Personality

All customers encounter personalities of the individuals who serve them and the overall personality or culture of the organization. The two are linked in that culture is a composite of many factors that strengthen and reinforce individual behavior. If a company is a fun place to work, its people will convey a sense of enjoyment to customers. If the culture is more formal, this, too, is reinforced by employee behaviors. If the culture is heavily sales-oriented, people will reflect behaviors common in salespeople; if the culture stresses meticulous attention to detail, employees will convey that to customers.

An organization's culture communicates to its customers.

Wal-Mart founder Sam Walton understood organizational behavior when he said, "Your people will treat your customers the way you [meaning managers] treat your people." Enthusiasm, comradeship, a sense of enjoyment, and humor quickly become evident to customers. Southwest Airlines, which has a culture of informality and promotes fun at work, projects an organizational personality very different from many of its competitors. This personality has been useful both in attracting customers and attracting employees.

The remainder of this chapter illustrates fifteen behaviors that convey personality. As you become aware of these behaviors, you'll quickly recognize A-plus opportunities in each. Awareness alone can improve service because, without awareness, employees may be essentially clueless as to the impact of these kinds of behaviors.[2]

Build A-Plus Personality by Treating Customers like Guests

The first impressions of your customer are important. The first few seconds of an encounter can set the stage for an ongoing relationship. Here are some ways to get off on the right foot.

Greet Your Customer Promptly

Woody Allen once said that 80 percent of success is just showing up. In customer service, 80 percent of success is treating the customer like a guest who just showed up.

When guests come to your home, you greet them, right? Yet we've all had the experience of being totally ignored by service people in some businesses. Never let a customer feel ignored.

A prompt greeting reduces the stress that customers feel when they find themselves on unfamiliar turf. Failing to greet would be like answering the doorbell at home, opening the front door, letting your guests into the foyer, and walking away without even acknowledging them. Anyone would feel awkward and uncomfortable in such a situation.

Studies have clocked the number of seconds customers waited to be greeted. Researchers then asked the people how long they'd been waiting. In every case, the customer's estimate of the time elapsed was much longer than the actual time. A wait of thirty or forty seconds can feel like three or four minutes. After just a few moments of being ignored, customers start thinking about going elsewhere.

Time drags when you're being ignored, and the customer will soon think about going elsewhere.

I once went to a watch repair shop where the repairman had a reputation for excellent work. His shop was tiny. I literally had to squeeze in behind another customer who was talking with the proprietor, who never looked at me, said hello, or acknowledged my presence. After a few minutes I decided to "come back later" because it felt awkward to wait in the shop while being ignored. Of course, I didn't come back and the repairman lost a customer simply because he failed to greet me.

Without prompt, friendly greetings, customers are unlikely to feel comfortable. So speak up. Verbally greet customers within ten seconds of the time they come into your business or approach your work location. Even if you are busy with another customer or on the phone, pause to say hello and let them know that you'll be ready to help them soon.

If you absolutely cannot say hello out loud or give undivided attention to a customer right away, you can make eye contact. Simply looking at your customers tells them much about your willingness to serve. Eye contact creates a bond between you and the customer. It conveys your interest in communicating further.

Get Your Customer Committed

Did you ever wonder why some fast-food restaurants send a clerk out to write your order on a sheet of paper while you are waiting in line? Think about it. You tell the person what you want and she marks it on a slip of paper, which she then gives back to you to present at the cash register where the order is called out. Why is this done? It is simply a way of getting the customer committed. If no one greeted you or wrote your order, you might be more likely to leave. Psychologically, you feel as if you've "ordered" so you stay in line and follow through with your lunch purchase.

Another way to get customers committed is to get them doing something. Telling your customers about your products or services isn't enough. They need to be doing something with your product.

///
Get the customer doing something as soon as possible.
///

Studies of the most successful computer salespeople, for example, show that they encourage customers to sit down at the computer as soon as possible to get them playing with it. They don't dazzle (or confuse) the customer with high-tech jargon or even information about the machine's capabilities. They get them doing something—perhaps play a video game or surf the net. Likewise, the best auto salespeople invite customers to sit in or test drive the car right away.

Other, less obvious ways to get people doing something and to engage their interest are to:

+ Personally hand them a shopping cart or basket.
+ Ask them to begin filling out paperwork (e.g., a customer survey or a contest entry form).
+ Get them to touch or sample the product.
+ Offer a cup of coffee, candy, or fruit while they wait.
+ Offer a product flyer, information packet, video presentation, or sample to review.

It doesn't matter so much what they do, as long as they begin to do something.

Build A-Plus Personality by Developing Rapport

Once you have greeted the customer, build rapport. Project your favorable personality with the following communication behaviors.

Smile Sincerely and Openly

As the old adage goes, Smile. It'll make people wonder what you've been up to. But more important, a smile tells customers that they came to the right place and are on friendly ground.

A genuine smile originates in two places, the mouth and the eyes. A lips-only version looks pasted on, insincere. It's like saying "cheese" when being photographed. It doesn't fool anyone. In fact, it might scare them away.

In fairness, some people smile more readily than others. For some a more serious facial expression is comfortable and natural. But in American culture, a smile is both expected and appreciated when one is meeting people. If you don't smile spontaneously, practice it. It need not be a Cheshire cat, ear-to-ear grin (in fact, that may really get people wondering about you), but just a pleasant, natural smile.

Incidentally, in some cultures smiling means something different. In Israel, for example, a clerk who smiles at customers is generally perceived as being inexperienced; in some Middle Eastern cultures, smiling is associated with a sexual come-on. But for most cultures, smiling is a rapport builder.

Break the Ice

The best way to start a conversation depends on what the customer needs. In many cases, customers need first to be reassured that the organization is a nice, friendly place to do business. Often customers want to browse and get the feel of the place before they commit to doing business. They need to dispel worries about being pressured into buying. This situation calls for the use of a nonthreatening icebreaker.

A good icebreaker for the browser can be an off-topic, friendly comment. Some options might be:

↳ *A Compliment.* For example, "That's a great-looking tie you're wearing," or "Your children are sure cute. How old are they?"

- *Weather-Related or Local Interest Comments.* For example, "Isn't this sunshine just beautiful?" or "Some snowfall, isn't it?" or "How about those Bulls last night?"
- *Small Talk.* Look for cues about the individual's interest in sports, jobs, mutual acquaintances, or past experiences, then initiate a relevant comment.

If the browsing customer seems to be focusing attention on a product (say he is holding several shirts or is looking at a particular product display), he can be reclassified as a focused shopper. The best icebreaker for the focused shopper is one that is more specific to the buying decision. In this case you want to make a comment that:

- *Anticipates the customer's questions* (e.g., "What size are you looking for, sir?" or "Can I help you select a —?")
- *Provides additional information* (e.g., "Those are all 25 percent off today," or "We have additional [name item] in the stock room.")
- *Offers a suggestion or recommendation* (e.g., "Those stripe suits are really popular this season," or "If you need help with measurements our estimators can figure out what you'll need.")

Be attentive to customers' needs. Give them time to browse if that is what they need, but be responsive to them in helping make a buying decision when they are ready to buy.

In nonretail organizations, use a friendly, sincere expression of willingness to serve. Asking how you can help works well.

Use appropriate icebreakers to establish rapport with customers.

Compliment Freely and Sincerely

It only takes a second to say something nice to a person, and it can add enormous goodwill. As with the icebreaker, a compliment may start with a comment on something people are wearing, their car, or their kids. In addition, complimenting someone's behavior can be a nice way to build rapport (e.g., "Thanks for waiting; you've been very patient," or "I noticed you checking the ————; you're a careful shopper," or "You seem to know a lot about ————; let's see if we can meet your needs").

Compliment people freely and sincerely. To get yourself in the habit of complimenting, try this: Set a goal to give ten sincere compliments each day. Make it a habit.

Call People by Name

A person's name is his or her favorite sound. We appreciate it when people make the effort to find out and use our names in addressing us. When appropriate, introduce yourself to your customers and ask their name. If this isn't appropriate (such as when you are waiting on a line of customers), you can often get a customer's name from a check, credit card, order form, or other paperwork.

Don't be overly familiar too quickly. You are normally safe calling people Mr. Smith or Ms. Jones, but it may be seen as rude if you call them Homer and Marge. (This is especially true when younger employees are dealing with older customers.) Better to err on the side of being too formal. If people prefer first-name address, they'll tell you so.

Be Sensitive to Timing and Follow-Up

Nothing impresses as significantly as immediate follow-through. Successful salespeople follow up with customers (usually by phone) to see that their purchases are satisfactory. Some salespeople do this occasionally when they have a little spare time; the more successful ones do it regularly at scheduled times. Likewise, the best customer-oriented people make commitments to customers and always follow up.

//

Customer follow-through builds stronger relationships and demonstrates personality.

//

Use a notebook or simple form to jot down follow-up commitments made to customers. Don't let these commitments drop through the cracks.

I have an insurance representative who calls me every year on my birthday and anniversary. He *never* fails. And although it's become a joke in our family that we'll hear from Ray on that day, he has been absolutely consistent for almost twenty years! That tells me something about his commitment to long-term relationships with his customers.

Reach Out and Touch Customers

Physical touch is a powerful form of communication. Take an opportunity to shake hands with a customer or even pat her on the back, if appropriate.

A study of bank tellers shows the power of touch. Tellers were taught to place change in the hand of the customer rather than place it on the counter. Researchers found that customer perceptions of the bank rose sharply among customers who had been touched. In a similar study, The Waiters Association tells members they can increase their tips by 42 percent by touching diners briefly on the shoulder when placing the tip tray on the table or on the palm when returning change.[3]

///
Restaurant servers who touch their customers earn higher tips.
///

Among internal customers and coworkers, a literal pat on the back can build instant rapport. But don't overdo it; some people resent people who seem too touchy-feely. Recognize different preferences. Try touching behavior, but be willing to adjust if the person seems uncomfortable or ill at ease. And, of course, the keyword here is *appropriateness*. Never touch a person in a manner that could be interpreted as overly intimate or having sexual overtones.

Build A-Plus Personality by Creating a Communication Circle

Good communication is circular, not one-directional. Use feedback and listening to build stronger relationships with customers. Try the tactics explained in the following sections.

Often Ask, How'm I Doing?

Legendary politician and former New York City mayor Ed Koch would constantly ask his constituents, "How'm I doing?" The phrase became his tag line. There is some evidence that he even listened to their answers. After all, he survived as mayor of the Big Apple for many years. Employees and managers can learn something from the Koch question.

Businesses need to ask how they are doing in as many ways as possible. In addition to more formalized measurement and feedback systems, employees need to demonstrate an attitude of receptiveness. Being receptive to the comments and criticisms of people is challenging and, at times, frustrating. It takes a lot of courage not only to accept criticism but to actually request it!

Nevertheless, some of your best ideas come from the correction others give you.

//
Always demonstrate an attitude of receptiveness; be willing to receive all kinds of feedback from customers.
//

Listen with More Than Your Ears

Since so few people are really good listeners, this skill provides an excellent A-plus opportunity. There is no such thing as an unpopular listener. Almost everyone becomes more interesting when he stops talking and starts listening. Pay attention to your talk-listen ratio. Are you giving the customer at least equal time?

To be a better listener, use and teach your employees these ideas:

→ *Judge the content of what people are saying, not the way they are saying it.* Customers may not have the right words, but they know what they need better than anyone.

→ *Hold your fire.* Don't jump to make judgments before your customer has finished talking.

→ *Work at listening.* Maintain eye contact and discipline yourself to listen to what is being said. Tune out those thoughts that get you thinking about something else.

→ *Resist distractions.* Make the customer the center of your attention.

→ *Seek clarification from customers.* Make sure you fully understand their needs. Do so in a nonthreatening way by using sincere, open-ended questions.

Say Please and Thank You

At the risk of sounding like one of those books that recite "things I learned in kindergarten," be polite. It may seem old-fashioned and some customers may not be as polite to you, but that's not their job.

I have noticed a disturbing trend among salespeople who say "There you go" to conclude a transaction. That kind of comment is not an appropriate substitute for thanking the customer. "Thank you" continues to be one of the most powerful phrases in human communication.

///
"There you go" is no substitute for "thank you."
///

Please and *thank you* are powerful words for building customer rapport and creating customer loyalty. They are easy to say and well worth the effort.

Reassure the Customer's Decision to Do Business with You

Buyer's remorse can set in pretty fast when people make large purchases. At the time of sale, you can inoculate against remorse by reassuring the customer that they've made a good purchasing decision.

Phrases such as, "I'm sure you'll get lots of enjoyment out of this" or "Your family will love it" can help reassure and strengthen the buyer's resolve to follow through with the purchase and, as important, feel good about it.

A powerful tool for reassuring customers is the telephone. One consulting approach for bank executives shows how important customer calls can be. As part of a training session, the executives develop a simple script and immediately go to the phones to call some of their customers. The conversation goes something like this:

> "Hello, I'm Chris Wilson from Major Bank. I just wanted to call to let you know that we appreciate your business and would be interested in any suggestions you might have for additional ways we could serve you."

That's it. Then they let the customer talk. The results: Customers are astounded that their banker would actually call and that he or she wasn't trying to sell anything. The image of the bank's service goes up sharply.

//
Reach out and listen to your customers.
//

Build A-Plus Personality with Good Telephone Techniques

Practice Good Telephone Behaviors

Telephone use calls for some special behaviors, especially if your only contact with customers is by the phone. A key to successful phone use is to simply remember that your customer cannot see you. Your challenge is to make up for all that lost nonverbal communication by using your voice effectively. Let's review a few key behaviors:

→ *Give the caller your name.* Let the caller know who you are just as you would in a face-to-face situation (i.e., when a name tag or desk plaque would identify you).

→ *Smile into the phone.* Somehow people can hear a smile over the phone. Some telephone pros place a mirror in front of them while they're on the phone to remind them that facial expression can transmit through the wires.

→ *Keep your caller informed.* If you need to look up information, tell the customer what you are doing. Don't leave them holding a dead phone with no clue as to whether you are still with them.

→ *Invite the caller to get to the point.* Use questions such as "How can I assist you today?" or "What can I do for you?"

→ *Commit to requests of the caller.* Tell the caller specifically what you will do and when you will get back to them (e.g., "I'll check on this billing problem and get back to you by five this afternoon, okay?").

→ *Thank the caller.* This lets the caller know when the conversation is over.

➔ *Let your voice fluctuate in tone, rate, and loudness.* You hold people's attention by putting a little life into your voice. Express honest reactions in expressive ways. Let your voice tones be natural and friendly.

➔ *Use hold carefully.* People hate being put on hold. When it's necessary, explain why and break in periodically to let them know they haven't been forgotten. If what you're doing will take longer than a few minutes, ask the caller if you can call back. Write down your commitment to call back and don't miss it.

➔ *Use friendly, tactful words.* Never accuse your customers of anything; never convey that their request is an imposition.[4]

Build A-Plus Personality by Enjoying People

The best customer service personalities convey a sense of enjoyment in their interaction with people. Yes, customers—other people—can be annoying at times, and sometimes the personalities clash, but, by and large, people are pleasant and interesting. Look for the positive in association with others.

Enjoy People and Their Diversity

J. D. Salinger said, "I am a kind of paranoid in reverse. I suspect people of plotting to make me happy." With an attitude like that we'd look forward to every meeting with every customer. Of course, we quickly learn that some customers do not seem to be plotting to make us happy. Most are very pleasant. Some are unusual. A few are downright difficult.

Every person is different; each has a unique personality. The kinds of people who tend to bug us the most are the ones who are not like us. Accept this diversity and learn to enjoy it. Know that peoples' needs are basically the same at some level and that treating them as guests will create the most goodwill, most of the time.

Work on Verbal Discipline

Confine your "self-talk"—those internal conversations in your mind— and your comments to others to focus on the positive, and avoid being judgmental. Instead of saying, "This kid has a really stupid haircut," say, in a nonjudgmental way, "Kids seem to enjoy looking different." Instead of saying, "This guy will nickel-and-dime me to death," say, "This customer is very cost-conscious."

//

Be careful to avoid judgmental, critical self-talk. It can come across to your customers.

//

At times you'll have to force yourself to avoid the negative and judgmental. Try making a game out of it. Sincerely try for one full day to avoid saying anything negative or judgmental about another person. If you make it through the day, shoot for another day. Verbal discipline can become a habit that pays off. You'll find yourself enjoying people more.

SELF-EVALUATION: HOW DOES YOUR PERSONALITY MEASURE UP?

Below is a list of the fifteen individual behaviors we've discussed in this chapter. Be completely honest in evaluating how well you feel you and your company employees do with each. After rating your people on the scale, go back through the list and circle the plus (+) or minus (-) to indicate how you feel about your response. If you are comfortable with your answer, circle the plus sign. If you wish you could honestly answer otherwise, circle the minus sign. These can provide topics for training and coaching employees.

For each of the following fifteen statements, answer:

N = Never; O = Occasionally; S = Sometimes;
M = Most of the time; A = Always

Our company employees:	N O S M A	+ −	*Goal*
1. Immediately greet all customers like guests.			
2. Use appropriate icebreakers to build rapport.			

Our company employees:	N O S M A	+ −	Goal
3. Compliment people freely and often			
4. Call customers by their names.			
5. Make and maintain good eye contact with customers.			
6. Often ask for feedback to find out how they're doing.			
7. Work hard to listen well.			
8. Always say please and thank you.			
9. Make it a point to reassure customers' decisions to do business with me.			
10. Smile freely and often.			
11. Use good telephone techniques.			
12. Work hard to give immediate follow-up with customers.			
13. Avoid letting commitments drop through the cracks.			
14. Use appropriate touching behaviors with customers when possible.			
15. Avoid expressing negative, judgmental comments about people.			

For each item where you circled a minus (-) sign, write a goal for improvement. Consider providing training or coaching sessions as well as ways to measure using structured observations.

Build A-Plus Personality with Organizational Culture

In addition to the individual behaviors described previously, customers also assess the personality of the entire organization by looking at group behaviors and attitudes. The communication rule that anything can and will convey a message still applies for these behaviors, of course. The composite result of group and individual behaviors conveys much about the culture of the organization. If the customer likes your culture, you are well on your way to A-plus personality and to building satisfaction and loyalty. Here are some organizational behaviors to consider.

//
Be aware of organizational culture elements that convey personality.
//

"Friendliness" of Organizational Systems

Fortune magazine columnist Stewart Alsop tells of spending forty-five minutes buying an upgrade to a plane ticket on America West Airlines. He wanted to pay extra for first-class seats for himself and his wife. The upgrade cost $250 per ticket, but "required the full attention of one of the two gate clerks, as well as assistance from the gate supervisor. Everyone else on the plane had to check in with the one other gate attendant, a process that—of course—took twice as long as usual. As they waited in line, they all could see that I was the one holding things up."

Alsop goes on to describe how the gate agent could not figure out how to respond to his request for the upgrade. She spent considerable time typing mysterious commands into her computer terminal and then talking to the terminal when it didn't do what she hoped it would. The gate supervisors had to help and the process even involved filling out carbon copy forms to serve as credit card receipts. He then summarizes the irony of the episode:

> Think about this: I was a customer who wanted to pay an extraordinarily high price (almost twice the original fare) for something that costs the airline little more than the price of a better snack. . . . I wanted to pay an extra $500 for the privilege of sitting in seats that, as it turned out, would have been empty anyway. The airline's response to this opportunity? Forcing me to stand in line and making me feel like a blithering idiot in front of my friends and spouse.[5]

Clumsy systems turn off customers and communicate unspoken messages. In this case, the customer received the message that he was a troublesome burden. This despite the fact that the airline stood to make additional money.

//

Clumsy systems that inconvenience people say that the organization doesn't care about customers.

//

The Company's Appearance and Grooming

From the moment we meet people, we begin to size them up. We begin to draw conclusions about them almost immediately. What we decide about their trustworthiness and ability is largely a factor of first impressions, and, of course, you only get one chance to make that first impression.

The appearance of an organization's employees is one of the first things seen by customers. Dress standards can set a company apart from the competition and create an A-plus experience. One way to approach dress standards is by looking at what other successful companies are doing. You need not be a copycat or wear an outfit you hate, but do consider what other role models do. And then meet or exceed their appearance.

An owner of an auto repair shop tried an experiment. All mechanics were paid on commission for the amount of repair work they brought in. The owner invited the mechanics to volunteer to change their dress and grooming. Several agreed to cut their hair shorter, shave daily, and wear clean uniforms. The outcome was a good example of A-plus: Those who improved their appearance generated far more repeat business than the others. The customers would ask for the better-dressed mechanics, and those who chose to dress and groom themselves in the "old way" found themselves getting less work.

Remember, of course, that the keyword in dress and grooming is appropriate. Salespeople in a surf shop would look foolish in three-piece suits; an undertaker would look ludicrous in a Hawaiian sport shirt. To overcome problems of individual differences that may be inappropriate, some organizations issue uniforms. These may be coveralls, full uniforms, or partial uniforms such as blazers, vests, or work shirts. Some employees like uniforms (they save on the costs of a wardrobe) while others resist the sameness of the uniformed look.

///
Appropriate dress and grooming convey nonverbal messages about the organization.
///

Determine what level of professionalism you want your people to convey to customers, then create a look that projects competence. Your customers notice these things.

Work Area Appearance

A cluttered work area conveys a sense of disorganization and low professionalism. Look around you and see what your customer sees. Is the place clean and tidy? Does the workspace look like an organized, efficient place? Is merchandise displayed attractively?

Check, too, for barriers. Often people arrange their workspace with a desk, counter, or table between them and the customer. While sometimes this is necessary, often it creates a barrier—both physical and psychological—between the customer and the employee. Encourage employees to invite customers to sit beside their desk instead of across from them. Consider using small round tables, especially when customers need to read materials given them. (Some auto dealerships have removed all sales office desks and replaced them with small round tables. Now the customer and salesperson sit around the table and work together to make a deal. Customers don't feel as if they are on opposite sides, in "combat" with the dealer, when the table is round.)

///
Look out for barriers created by furniture arrangements or company layout.
///

Finally, look for customer comfort. Are your customers invited to sit in a comfortable chair? Do your offices or stores invite them to relax? Are waiting areas furnished with reading materials or perhaps a TV? Are vending machines available? Is the vending area kept clean?

A small auto body shop I visited surprised me. It had a waiting room that resembled a living room in a nice home. There were easy chairs, a TV, a coffee table adorned with recent magazines, even fresh flowers.

Recently, more auto dealers have begun to emphasize ways to make their car lots and showrooms, many of which are decades old, more attractive and customer-friendly. Some now feature landscaped settings with benches and pathways, different display areas for each auto brand, and interactive systems with screens that show how elements like paint colors and upholstery look together. Take a look at your work areas from the customer's viewpoint.[6]

Organizational Listening

At the heart of any efforts to win customer loyalty is listening to customers. Companies that do this well A-plus their customers with positive organizational personality. Most highly successful companies employ some of the following ideas, and a few use them all. Average and poorly performing companies either use few of these ideas or do a poor job of incorporating the feedback received into their customer service strategies. Five categories of A-plus listening are:[7]

1. *Using customer satisfaction indices.* Surveying customers about their level of satisfaction and plotting the results can provide valuable feedback. Since most surveys use quantitative data, results can be compared over time to identify trends. The best surveys are ones that allow customers to identify their areas of concern. By taking this feedback seriously, we demonstrate a willingness to listen to our customers.

2. *Soliciting feedback.* The most valuable feedback we get is the customer complaint. While most people don't like being criticized, the fact is that only through such criticism can meaningful changes be made. A-plus companies do a good job of soliciting feedback—especially complaints—on product and service quality.

3. *Expanding market research.* Although companies traditionally invest significantly in this area, they often overlook two critical listening points. Customers should be interviewed both at the time of arrival (when they become customers) and at the time of departure (when they defect) about the reasons for their behavior. A-plus companies ask cus-

tomers about their needs, how they heard about the company, what characteristics they are looking for in a company like theirs, and what sparked their decision to use the company's products. Careful questioning of departing customers can isolate those attributes that are causing customers to leave and can demonstrate goodwill while making a last ditch attempt to keep the customer. One company found that it recaptured a full 35 percent of its defectors just by contacting them and listening to them earnestly.

4. *Training and rewarding frontline employees.* Employees who have direct contact with customers have a superb opportunity to demonstrate organizational listening. Train people to listen effectively (don't assume people can do this spontaneously) and to make the first attempts at amends for the customer who has a bad experience. Make sure employees have ways of capturing the information and passing it along to the rest of the company. Often a simple complaint log works well. Forms or computer screens with categories of customer complaints can also help digest the data received and pass it to people who can best fix the problem.

5. *Involving the customer.* Customers who engage in experiences with the company feel a part of the action and feel as if they've been listened to. Southwest Airlines actually invites frequent fliers to its first round of interviews with prospective flight attendants and considers those customers' opinions in the hiring process. Creative companies invite prospective customers to participate in new-product development sessions. This is a powerful form of listening that projects an A-plus personality.

///
Constantly look for ways to "listen" to customer concerns with a variety of media.
///

Regular Communication

Use routine notes of thanks to keep communication channels open. A week after purchasing running shoes, the customers of one small shop receive handwritten notes from the store owner thanking them for buying. The note simply expresses appreciation for their business and invites them to return. No fancy prose, a one- or two-sentence message is all that's needed.

An airport car rental agency has employees write thank you notes to customers when the desk is not busy. The notes are handwritten on the company letterhead and personalized to mention the type of car rented. They thank customers and invite them to rent again the next time they are in town. The cost of doing this is practically nil, since the desk is busy when flights are coming in but then has slow periods in between. Why have employees waste time when business is slow? Use that time to communicate with customers. These are some simple ways to not let your customer forget you. A quick thank you is always appreciated.

Other ways to keep communication open are to send customers information about upcoming sales, changes in policies, or new promotions. A print shop sends all customers a monthly package of coupons, flyers, and samples, including a printed motivational quotation on parchment paper suitable for framing. Additional copies of the quote are available free for the asking. The mailing acts as a reminder of the quality of work the shop can do as well as a promotion. Keep the customer tied in with mailings, e-mail updates, or phone contact.

Staying Close after the Sale

Customers hate a love-'em-and-leave-'em relationship. Yet many companies offer just that. Once the sale is made the customer goes back to feeling like a stranger. Look for opportunities to contact the customer after the sale. Establish an ongoing friendship and they'll keep coming back.

Some ideas for connecting with customers after the sale include:

- ✦ Sending thank you notes or other goodwill follow-up
- ✦ Adding customers to an e-mail distribution list
- ✦ Calling or e-mailing to be sure the product/service met their needs
- ✦ Sending out new-product information
- ✦ Sending clippings of interest or newsworthy information that may reassure customers that they made a good purchasing decision
- ✦ Sending birthday and holiday cards
- ✦ Inviting customers to participate in a focus group
- ✦ Calling to thank them for referrals

Using Hoopla and Fun

People enjoy working in an organization where they have fun. Successful companies have regular rituals that everyone gets involved in, whether it's Friday afternoon popcorn, birthday parties, or employee-of-the-month celebrations. Excellent organizations are fun places to work; they create rituals of their own.

As a manager at a utility company, I initiated frequent sales contests, complete with skits and prizes. Each time a particular product was sold, the service representative could pop a balloon and find inside a prize ranging from a $10 bill to a coupon good for a piece of pie in the company cafeteria. Employees loved it and got involved. The following ideas are easy and may be worthwhile to implement:

→ Employee (or hero) of the week/month recognition
→ Awards luncheons (include some tongue-in-cheek "awards")
→ Win-a-day-off-with-pay contests
→ Casual dress days
→ Halloween costume day
→ Family picnics

Don't fall into the trap of thinking that these activities are hokey. Employees at all levels enjoy celebrations and hoopla, and their effect spreads to the customer.

Build A-Plus Personality by Developing and Rewarding Employees

Ultimately, it is your employees who project organizational personality. No decisions are more important to a company than hiring and staffing decisions. Build A-plus personality by hiring smart and rewarding employees who demonstrate the right behaviors in serving customers.

Hiring Smart

Hire and promote people on the basis of their attitude and people skills. We all experience service people who just naturally seem to click with people. When you come across such people, make a note to contact them about possible work with you. Make shopping for employees an ongoing activity.

You can always teach people the technical skills needed to do a job. The people skills are tougher. Employees with a natural feel for communicating with people can be worth their weight in gold to your company.

Rewarding the Right Actions

Fairly often, organizations inadvertently reward one behavior while hoping for something else. In all too many cases an organization hopes something will happen but actually rewards an opposite behavior. For example, a company rewards individuals and departments for never receiving complaints. The hope is that by receiving no complaints it means we are doing a good job. The reality, however, may well be that no complaints are heard because the complaints are simply being suppressed. Customers have no effective way to voice a complaint. Instead, they just quit doing business with the company.

As we discussed in Chapter 3, it's not bad news to receive a complaint; it is bad news to suppress a complaint. Some percentage of customers will always be less than satisfied and ignoring them does no good. Quite the contrary. It makes sense to draw out those customer concerns so that they can be addressed and corrected.

Here are some other examples of possible reward conflicts where the wrong behaviors may be rewarded and the right behaviors ignored:

> ➔ *Rewarding employees for fast transaction handling when the customer may be left uninformed or may resent being rushed along.* Examples: The restaurant that encourages employees to get the customer fed and out may create unhappy customers who prefer to eat in a more relaxed environment. Another unsatisfied customer may be the electronic equipment buyer who does not understand how to work the features of his VCR before he leaves the store.

> ➔ *Encouraging salespeople to "cooperate with each other to best meet customer needs" while paying a straight commission.* Example: Salespeople practically trip over each other to approach the new customer before the next salesperson gets her.

→ *Encouraging employees to send thank you notes to customers but never allowing on-the-job time to do so.* This creates the impression that the thank you really isn't that important.

→ *Constantly stressing the need to reduce the amount of return merchandise by docking the pay of clerks who accept too many returns.* The result: Customers encounter reluctance to take back unsatisfactory products.

→ *Paying people by the hour instead of by the task accomplished.* Hourly wages are simpler to administer, but they basically pay people for using up time!

///
Check your organization. Are you really rewarding the right behaviors?
///

The reward system within an organization needs to be tilted to the advantage of the employee who provides excellent service. Any rewards should be given in direct relationship to the employee's contribution to customer service consistent with the theme you've selected.

Management is only limited by its imagination when it comes to rewarding employees. But the most important point is that managers must reward the right actions and results.

A Final Thought

Individual and organizational behaviors are conveyed to customers by little things. Often people are unaware of how they are coming across and, as such, are at a distinct disadvantage. Broadening our awareness of how other people read our verbal and nonverbal messages is a useful step in improving customer service.

Likewise, just as individuals project their behaviors to customers, so do organizations. The company's collective behavior patterns constitute its culture and may be perceived as favorable or unfavorable by customers (both internal and external customers). The ways managers and leaders interact with subordinates and associates have considerable impact on the way all people behave toward customers.

Self-Evaluation: Measure Your A-Plus Personality Efforts

Measure your results by interviewing ten or more customers of your business or organization. Follow the interview questionnaire presented here word for word. Ask each respondent to answer "yes," "no," or "unsure/ not applicable." Tabulate the results, giving two points for each "yes" response, and one point for each "N/A." Total the points, and divide the number by the number of questions answered. (If a question does not apply to your business, drop it.)

A score of 25 or lower on individual behaviors, or 10 or lower on organizational behaviors should be considered a red flag that immediate attention to that aspect of customer service is needed.

Repeat the evaluation periodically and compare the results against the last measure. The total score received, however, is less important than the direction of improvement. Applying the ideas in this book should help your scores increase.

Repeat a series of interviews every three months to identify changes, trends, or concerns.

Individual Behaviors Questionnaire

When you last did business with [name of company or department], did the employees there:

Yes   No   N/A

1. Greet you promptly?
2. Use opening comments to help you feel at ease?
3. Compliment you in any way?
4. Call you by your name?
5. Make and maintain eye contact with you?
6. Ask for feedback from you in any way?
7. Listen carefully to your needs or wants?
8. Say please and thank you?
9. Reassure you of your decision to do business with them?
10. Smile freely and often?
11. Use good telephone techniques?
12. Show a sensitivity to timing and follow up with you?

	Yes	No	N/A

13. Appropriately touch you (e.g., with a handshake, pat on back)?
14. Seem to enjoy people and their diversity?
15. Seem to have good attitudes about selling?
16. Keep the work place clean and attractive?
17. Dress and groom themselves appropriately?
18. Seem to enjoy working for this company?

Organizational Behaviors Questionnaire

When you last did business with [name of company or department], did the organization seem to:

	Yes	No	N/A

1. Use systems that make doing business easy?
2. Employ people who present an attractive, clean, and tidy appearance?
3. Have attractive, uncluttered, and clean offices, work areas, or showrooms?
4. Listen to your specific concerns and give you convenient opportunities to provide feedback?
5. Want to maintain ongoing communication with you as a customer?
6. Reward its employees who give good service?

WORKSHEETS:
SHOWING CUSTOMERS A-PLUS PERSONALITY

✍ TREATING CUSTOMERS LIKE GUESTS

Use this form to brainstorm possible A-plus ideas for treating customers like guests when they initially come into your business, department, or organization. Working alone or with a small group, jot down as many ideas as possible without regard for whether they are practical or immediately usable. Then review all ideas for possible adoption by your organization. Put a checkmark next to the ones you want to try.

☐
☐
☐
☐
☐

Develop a priority list indicating when you will apply each selected idea. Describe tasks or resources necessary to enact the A-plus ideas.

Ways to Treat Customers like
Guests   *Implementation Requirements*

1.   Time Frame:

                                          Tasks:

                                          Task Responsibility:

2.   Time Frame:

                                          Tasks:

                                          Task Responsibility:

3.   Time Frame:

                                          Tasks:

                                          Task Responsibility:

☞ DEVELOPING RAPPORT

Use this form to brainstorm possible A-plus ideas for developing rapport with your customers. Working alone or with a small group, jot down as many ideas as possible without regard for whether they are practical or immediately usable. Then review all ideas for possible adoption by your organization. Put a checkmark next to the ones you want to try.

☐
☐
☐
☐
☐

Develop a priority list indicating when you will apply each selected idea. Describe tasks or resources necessary to enact the A-plus ideas.

Ways to Develop Rapport	*Implementation Requirements*
1.	Time Frame:
	Tasks:
	Task Responsibility:
2.	Time Frame:
	Tasks:
	Task Responsibility:
3.	Time Frame:
	Tasks:
	Task Responsibility:

CREATING A COMMUNICATION CIRCLE

Use this form to brainstorm possible A-plus ideas for creating a communication circle with your customers. Working alone or with a small group, jot down as many ideas as possible without regard for whether they are practical or immediately usable. Then review all ideas for possible adoption by your organization. Put a checkmark next to the ones you want to try.

☐

☐

☐

☐

☐

Develop a priority list indicating when you will apply each selected idea. Describe tasks or resources necessary to enact the A-plus ideas.

Ideas for Creating Customer Communication Circles	*Implementation Requirements*
1.	Time Frame:
	Tasks:
	Task Responsibility:
2.	Time Frame:
	Tasks:
	Task Responsibility:
3.	Time Frame:
	Tasks:
	Task Responsibility:

PRACTICING BETTER TELEPHONE TECHNIQUES

Use this form to brainstorm possible A-plus ideas for using the telephone more effectively with your customers. Working alone or with a small group, jot down as many ideas as possible without regard for whether they are practical or immediately usable. Then review all ideas for possible adoption by your organization. Put a checkmark next to the ones you want to try.

☐
☐
☐
☐
☐

Develop a priority list indicating when you will apply each selected idea. Describe tasks or resources necessary to enact the A-plus ideas.

Better Phone Techniques	*Implementation Requirements*
1.	Time Frame:
	Tasks:
	Task Responsibility:
2.	Time Frame:
	Tasks:
	Task Responsibility:
3.	Time Frame:
	Tasks:
	Task Responsibility:

✍ ENJOYING ASSOCIATION WITH CUSTOMERS

Use this form to brainstorm possible A-plus ideas for enjoying work with your customers. Working alone or with a small group, jot down as many ideas as possible without regard for whether they are practical or immediately usable. Then review all ideas for possible adoption by your organization. Put a checkmark next to the ones you want to try.

☐

☐

☐

☐

☐

Develop a priority list indicating when you will apply each selected idea. Describe tasks or resources necessary to enact the A-plus ideas.

Ways to Enjoy Contact with Customers	*Implementation Requirements*
1.	Time Frame:
	Tasks:
	Task Responsibility:
2.	Time Frame:
	Tasks:
	Task Responsibility:
3.	Time Frame:
	Tasks:
	Task Responsibility:

Notes

1. Dave Barry, "Booth Won't Take Toll, but Bad Attitude Will," Knight-Ridder Newspapers, April 7, 1991. Reprinted with permission.
2. Many of the ideas in this section are adapted from P. Timm, *50 Powerful Ideas You Can Use to Keep Your Customers*, 2nd ed. (Hawthorne, N.J.: Career Press, 1995). Copyright Paul R. Timm.
3. "Tipping Tips," *The Wall Street Journal* (August 27, 1996), p. A1.
4. An excellent thirty-minute videotape training program featuring the author is *Winning Telephone Techniques* produced by JWA Video in Chicago. For information, call 312-829-5100.
5. Stewart Alsop, "My Trip on America West, or Why Customer Service Still Matters," *Fortune* (November 22, 1999), p. 359.
6. "A Picnic in a Car Lot?" *The Wall Street Journal* (October 13, 1994), p. A1.
7. Ideas were adapted from Thomas O. Jones and W. Earl Sasser, Jr., "Why Satisfied Customers Defect," *Harvard Business Review* (November–December 1995), p. 93.

Chapter 8

Strategy 7: Give Customers A-Plus Convenience

A slew of dot-com companies are spending millions to construct delivery networks that can ferry virtually anything to any home. . . . If they succeed, they could revolutionize the way Americans shop—and how they expect to be served.
—Douglas A. Blackmon, journalist[1]

The Way It Is . . .

Marcia was a regular customer at the Perimeter Center Publix Supermarket in Atlanta. During the busy Christmas holiday season she discovered a delicious low-fat eggnog. After trying it, she came back for more only to discover the store was out.

A chat with the dairy section employee brought promises that more product would be coming in soon. But when she returned to the store a day later, the product was again out of stock. This time the employee said, "More is coming in tomorrow and I'll set some aside for you." When she returned the next day the delivery truck had been late and, again, she went home with no eggnog.

This time the employee offered her A-plus convenience. He apologized and told her that as soon as the delivery came in, he would set some aside for her and deliver it to her home on his way home from work!

Home delivery! What a concept. A generation ago, home delivery of milk and other products was commonplace. In the early twenty-first century it may be making a comeback. Online grocery delivery services such as PeaPod and Net Grocer are reintroducing consumers to a level of convenience not often found in today's business world.

Enhancing speed and convenience for customers is a critical tactic. E-commerce sites live and die by their speed and responsiveness. Traditional businesses build great loyalty among customers who value the ways they respect their time and try to provide easy shopping.

A-Plus Convenience: What It Is

Customer convenience arises from speed of service and ease of doing business. Organizations that strive for efficient, easy-to-use services capture customer loyalty.

Let's look first at the first component, speed. Surpassing what the customer anticipates about speed may be one of the simplest yet most powerful ways of building customer loyalty. The ubiquitous convenience store (c-store) personifies key elements that can be applied to other businesses. C-stores allow parking at the door, reasonable selection, quick self-service, and out-the-door-in-a-minute service. Pay-at-the-pump gas dispensing makes things even quicker for many such stores.

The reason that people like such stores is simple: People today value time, perhaps more than ever before. Unfortunately, aside from convenience stores, many companies are far too casual about wasting customers' time.

We live in a world of commerce where we expect nearly instant gratification. We see things on the Web, order them, and fully expect that they will arrive on our doorstep in a day or two. When they do, we are likely to reorder; if the merchant fails to make the promised deadline, we are likely to be disappointed and will quit shopping with that company in favor of one that hustles a bit more.

///

Many companies overpromise and underdeliver when it comes to speed of service. They simply take longer than the customer has been led to expect.

///

Despite this, many companies still fall into the trap of overpromising and underdelivering. They make vague or unfulfilled commitments involving their customers' time. Here are a few examples:

→ A major computer distributor in Europe tells the customer that its mainframe will be restored to service "soon." The customer thought that "soon" meant twenty minutes or so; to the technician, "soon" meant about eight hours.

→ Some phone or cable companies routinely tell customers that they will be at their home to install service "between 7:30 A.M. and 5 P.M." on a given date. The customer is expected to sit around all day waiting for the installation.

→ A medical clinic hired me to survey patient satisfaction. Overwhelmingly, the most common complaint was that patients had to wait too long for the doctor. Customers felt that doctors had little regard for the value of their time. The result was a negative spiral where patients showed up later than the appointment time, figuring that the doctor would be late. The clinic then scheduled even more slack into the system and the situation got worse.

→ VitaminShoppe.com makes a big deal of offering to overnight products so the customer will have them the next day (at no extra charge, according to one promotion). But the merchandise doesn't show up for five days and the opportunity to A-plus a customer is long gone. So is the customer, in many cases.

On a more positive note, a number of businesses are built on the simple premise of giving A-plus speed and convenience. Federal Express promises package delivery "by 10:30 A.M." when it knows it can have the package there by 9:30 or 9:45. Customers are routinely surprised because most businesses fail to meet their own deadlines, thus showing disrespect for the customer's time. Likewise, when I worked for Xerox Corporation we used a similar practice. When customers called for a technician to fix their copy machine, we promised that someone would be at their office by two o'clock when we knew the service rep would be there by 1:30. This never failed to pleasantly surprise clients.

//
Consistently beating a time deadline provides customers with A-plus speed and convenience.
//

The Disney amusement parks create A-plus speed by having signs that tell visitors how long it will take to get to the ride from a given point in a cue. They have actually scheduled in a little fat. The lines inevitably move more quickly and customers are pleasantly surprised. A restaurant that tells patrons a table will be available in fifteen minutes and then seats them in ten will be far more popular than one promising fifteen minutes and delivering an eighteen- or twenty-minute wait for seating.

How to Produce A-Plus Convenience

We can provide A-plus convenience and speed by ensuring that several actions become ongoing ways of doing business:

- → Seriously value our customers' time.
- → Make things easier for our customers.
- → Create once-and-done service.
- → Make doing business with us easy.
- → Offer ancillary services.

As with any A-plus tactic, companies need to be ever-vigilant to ways of improving systems and behaviors that can enhance convenience. If you don't offer better and better convenience, your competition will. Customers are screaming for it, and you need to provide it.

///
Customers are constantly demanding enhanced convenience.
///

Give Serious Regard to Customer Time and Convenience

Time is a valuable commodity to your customers. When we disregard it or fail to share our customers' sense of urgency, we discount our customer. Few things are more frustrating than waiting for something that seems to take longer than necessary. In fact, of all the pet peeves identified in my research and described by seminar participants, slow service is at or near the top of everyone's list.

Speed is easier to work with than convenience. In fact, the nice thing about creating A-plus speed is that you have control. You can clearly create the expectation by telling customers how long things will take.

Once the customer anticipates a particular time period, you can simply beat it.

Make sure customers get a realistic perception of how long it takes to complete a transaction or process or to deliver your product or service. I heard from a nurse in a hospital that was a client of mine of a situation where a patient was sent to the blood lab for a blood test. The phlebotomist drew the blood sample and took it behind a curtain to be sent off for analysis. Upon returning to the patient, the technician was asked by the patient what the results of the test were. The lab technician laughed and explained that the test was to be done at another facility and results would not be ready until the next day. The point: Customers don't always know how long things take. You need to tell them.

///

Customers often don't know how long things take. You need to advise them and, in so doing, set the expectation.

///

Too many businesses fall to the temptation to promise quicker service and hope for the best. They hate to deliver unpleasant news, so, instead, offer a time frame that sounds good but cannot be delivered realistically. In doing so they miss a significant opportunity to underpromise and overdeliver. It is better to give a realistic time you can beat rather than a pie-in-the-sky estimate you cannot meet.

In addition to showing regard for their customers' time, companies need to think about time's cousin, which is customer convenience. Offering A-plus convenience is one of the most powerful ways to build loyalty. This is easily illustrated by looking at two kinds of businesses that have flourished because they were built around A-plus convenience:

→ *Takeout.* The most popular restaurant food in America is pizza. In the late 1950s, when pizza was gaining widespread popularity across the country, it was served just like any other restaurant entree. People ordered their pizza, waited fifteen or twenty minutes for it to be baked, and ate it at the restaurant. Then came the convenience pioneers like Domino's Pizza. Early in the life of this pizza chain, it made the strategic decision to focus exclusively on takeout (what Europeans call "take away") and on delivery service.

The strategy was a hit. People came to associate Domino's with the thirty-minute delivery guarantee; in turn, Domino's and its competitors taught Americans a new way of buying restaurant food. Since then, countless pizza chains and independent restaurants have followed that model. Today, meals prepared outside the home account for nearly half the U.S. food-dollar spending. The Food Marketing Institute says that "Americans want to spend no more than fifteen minutes preparing a meal. . . . Today's shoppers want their food and they want it now." Seven out of ten households buy "home meal replacements" (otherwise known as takeout) at least once a month.[2]

Of course, the choices now go far beyond pizza or restaurant meals alone. Supermarkets and delis provide a wide range of prepared meals that need nothing more than heating and eating. Food producers are packaging ingredients together so consumers can prepare complete meals without having to buy each ingredient separately. Shredded potatoes, chopped peppers, onions, and diced ham are provided in separate plastic bags within a box describing the meal. Pizza crusts are sold with packets of topping; prepared sandwiches are packaged with chips and a cookie to make an instant box lunch. All these efforts are attempts to meet the customer's need for convenience.

///
Products packaged together allow customers the convenience of not having to shop for separate ingredients.
///

→ *Quick-Lube Shops.* Another classic convenience breakthrough is the stand-alone automobile oil change business that emerged in the late 1970s and the 1980s. Before companies like Jiffy Lube, Q Lube, and Minute Man, auto owners needing an oil change typically took their car to a dealership or gas station. They dropped it off, caught a ride to work, returned after work, and picked up their car. It could easily be an all-day deal and was pretty inconvenient. Then came the quick-lube shop.

Today, we go to a Jiffy Lube or similar shop and have a cup of coffee in a customer lounge while a team of technicians pounces on our car, changes the oil, checks the tires and all fluids, and vacuums the inside. The whole process takes ten or fifteen minutes. This is A-plus convenience.

Make Things Easier for Customers

Another way businesses provide A-plus service is by taking the hassle out of cumbersome systems. Unnecessary paperwork is an area where many companies can improve. Smart companies regularly look at the forms or applications customers need to complete and determine if these are all really necessary. They check for redundancy or requests for unnecessary information that may be making the paperwork process more difficult than it needs to be. Some of the better mortgage or consumer loan companies make the application process streamlined by pre-completing parts of the paperwork. For example, a credit union mortgage department I recently worked with downloaded all my relevant credit and account information before giving me forms to complete. I needed to fill out only a few lines.

Likewise, a used auto dealership I bought from had all the information about the car preprinted on the sales documents. The sales representative slipped a few forms into his computer printer and the otherwise-complicated paperwork was reduced to a matter of a few signatures.

By contrast, I recently had the unpleasant experience of filling out some forms for a healthcare provider. Each form required me to reenter my name, address, telephone number, Social Security number, and such. It got annoying.

Repetitious or unnecessary paperwork is annoying. Make life easier for your customer by simplifying forms and applications.

Look at your organization to determine if you are requiring repetitive busywork from your customers, then A-plus them by eliminating it.

Create Once-and-Done Service

"That's not my department" may be one of the least-favorite phrases for customers. Likewise, having to repeatedly tell a story to person after person while seeking a solution drives customers nuts. Strive for once-and-done service. Make it easy for customers to get everything they need and any problem solved at a single place.

The Ritz-Carlton Hotel Company is well known for its simple employee position—that Ritz-Carlton employees are "ladies and gentlemen serving ladies and gentlemen." When a hotel guest asks any employee for something, that employee "owns" that request or problem until it is fulfilled or solved. If a guest asks a maid where she can get a copy of a foreign language newspaper, the maid will either get the paper for her or find out where the guest can get it. The maid is empowered to take the time to run to a newsstand if that will get the guest what she wants. That's once-and-done service. And it blows customers away. This hotel chain won the prestigious Malcolm Baldrige National Quality Award in part because of such an exceptional service philosophy.

At the heart of once-and-done service is employee willingness and ability to take responsibility for meeting needs and reducing customer inconvenience. Strong companies hire people with initiative and empower them to do whatever the customer needs. I'll talk more in Chapter 9 about the importance of empowering and motivating employees.

Make Doing Business Easy

A *Wall Street Journal* article in November 1999 revealed a "secret weapon" used by discount retailers to "once again trounce traditional department stores. Was it sophisticated pricing, the latest in-store design, or cutting-edge inventory management? Actually, after twenty years of growing discounter dominance, a simpler explanation rolls into view: the shopping cart."

The article goes on to say that the impact of something as simple as a shopping cart is significant. A marketing research firm found that "the average shopper with a cart buys 7.2 items, while the customer without a cart buys 6.1. "As old-fashioned as they seem, carts are perfectly suited for the way people shop today: They're pressed for time and buy more in fewer trips. Mothers struggling to corral children love them. The growing ranks of senior citizens lean on carts for support and appreciate not having to carry their purchases."[3]

///
Simple things like shopping carts and convenient store location can enhance customer loyalty.
///

Shopping malls are beginning to recognize the importance of making shopping easier. Worried about competition from point-and-click e-commerce sites, mall developers are working to cluster similar stores together so customers can comparison shop.

The traditional mall was designed to be difficult. Retailers wanted people to wander through the malls to increase exposure to other stores. The more the customer walks, the greater the chance he or she will find something else to buy. But e-commerce is changing this, too. People want to compare prices and selection at similar stores and they don't want to have to walk far to do it. (After all, they can do it very easily online.) Many frustrated, time-pressed shoppers have already defected from malls to big-box discounters (e.g., Wal-Mart, Kmart, Target, Home Depot) where they can get everything they need in one place.[4]

Offer Ancillary Services

Loblaw's Supermarkets, Canada's largest chain, offers an ever-growing range of ancillary services to its shoppers. Its latest innovation at a new Toronto store is a complete for-women-only fitness club equipped with saunas, tanning beds, and daycare center. The club offers everything from treadmills to Tae-Bo classes—all just steps from the produce aisle. *The Wall Street Journal* reports that "like many grocery-store chains, Loblaw rents store space to dry cleaners, liquor stores, coffee shops, and has in-house pharmacies and banking centers. But few chains carry the concept as far as Loblaw does. [T]he chain has started offering video-game and cell-phone sales outlets in some of its stores. In addition it began leasing space to the Club Monoco Inc. clothing store chain and teaching community cooking lessons in stores."[5]

Such ancillary services create A-plus convenience for the chain's customers while providing one-stop shopping for almost every need.

Simplify the Product

The running joke about people being unable to program a video cassette recorder indicates the constant need to simplify products for exceptional ease of use—and convenience. The computer industry has made quantum leaps with plug-and-play technology, but still has a ways to go. The newly emerging market for "information appliances" opens new possibilities. Information appliances are simplified computers that buyers can plug in and hook up to the Internet. They don't have the computing power of PCs, but most users never need it. They allow users to surf the Net and use e-mail without the complicated processes associated with setting up a typical PC. And, of course, they cost a lot less.

///
Simplification of products sold can improve customer convenience and win loyalty.
///

On a more mundane level, product packaging is responding to the customer's desire for convenience. The newest Kellogg cereal, Special K plus, is packaged in a resealable box that looks like a half-gallon milk carton. It contains the same amount of cereal as larger, more cumbersome boxes but stores it in less space and is easy to pour.

SELF-EVALUATION: MEASURE YOUR A-PLUS CONVENIENCE EFFORTS

As with any measurement, the critical element is to understand the customer's point of view. Try using mystery shoppers. This technique will help you evaluate the speed and convenience the average customer experiences.

Mystery shopping is a process whereby companies send researchers who act like customers to gather information about the customer experience. After visiting a business, your "shoppers" should be able to tell you answers to these kinds of questions:

1. *How long do customer contacts take?* Use a stopwatch to calculate average times for a variety of transactions. Chart these times after any changes are made in procedures or policies.

Remember, however, it may not be the absolute amount of time but rather the customer's perception of time that is important. You can better measure this if you ask a customer how long he or she had to wait for a service, then compare this time with the actual time observed. Customers typically report a time that's longer than the actual service wait.

Be careful, however, not to rush a customer when more leisurely, personalized service may be the standard you seek. A gourmet restaurant does not push its customer to chow down and get moving. Likewise, some stores seem to savor their customer-contact time. For example, Kiehl's Since 1851, Inc., is a little New York company, almost 150 years old, that makes and sells hair- and skin-care products for men and women. While competitors push product out the door, Kiehl's philosophy of business is different. The company intentionally keeps its business small to preserve its brand of customer service. At the Kiehl's store, the staff is famous for spending a half-hour with one customer. While a long line waits, the employee grills customer after customer about skin- and hair-care characteristics and then disgorges detailed information about the products.[6]

2. *How easy is your telephone system?* A persistent pet peeve is a clumsy telephone system. Call your own company to hear for yourself how good or bad your phone menus are. For example:

→ Can you get to a live person at any time? Does the caller know what to do to get out of the automated menu labyrinth and get a real person on the line?

→ Are you requesting too much information from customers before they get to speak with someone? Do you really need their account number, for example?

→ Do you offer too many choices (more than four, typically, would be too many) for customers to remember?

3. *Do you currently offer delivery, immediate faxing, instantaneous e-mail responses, or the like?* If not, would such options be possibilities your company could consider?

4. *Do you know what kinds of conveniences your competitors are offering?* If not, send an explorer group (as discussed in Chapter 4) to visit them and learn what they are doing.

A Final Thought

Customers are easily surprised by efficient service that goes beyond what they anticipate. Likewise, they appreciate anything that can make life easier for them. This need has spun off some pretty innovative time-savers such as drive-in mortuaries, quickie-wedding chapels, and the like. While those examples may carry the principle further than most of us want to go, they do reflect the almost universal desire for efficient, timely service with a minimum of inconvenience.

And don't forget the "little things" principle. The little things can make big differences. I saw an example of this during the busy Christmas season when a package shipping store sent a greeting card to all its customers and included with it a shipping form, so the customer could fill it out in advance when bringing in a package next time. Another little touch is restaurant servers who don't make customers wait for their check or for beverage refills, but instead anticipate the diners' needs and meet them promptly.

Serving up beverage refills without the customer having to ask provides a convenience that is easy to give and is much appreciated by customers.

As you look for convenience opportunities, here's one word of warning: Be careful of innovations that may work at cross-purposes. A comment in *Business Week* illustrates an unintended consequence of providing convenient information:

> Is it advertising run amok? Movie trailers have come to your ATM. And more may be on the way. Full-motion video ads are now running on the screens of automated teller machines at some 7-Eleven stores. . . . Customers have already seen coming attractions for some films at the convenience store. And who knows? You may see that *Star Wars* trailer at your local savings and loan. Hold it, aren't those lines slow enough already?[7]

Constantly look for opportunities to exceed what your customer has come to anticipate with regard to speed and convenience.

WORKSHEETS:
GIVING CUSTOMERS A-PLUS CONVENIENCE

✍ PAYING ATTENTION TO CUSTOMER TIMING

Use this form to brainstorm possible A-plus convenience ideas. How might your organization better provide customers with efficient, speedy service? Working alone or with a small group, jot down as many ideas as possible without regard for whether they are practical or immediately usable. Then review all ideas for possible adoption by your organization. Put a checkmark next to the ones you want to try.

☐
☐
☐
☐
☐

Develop a priority list indicating when you will apply each selected idea. Describe tasks or resources necessary to enact the A-plus ideas.

How to Show Sensitivity to
Customers' Time   *Implementation Requirements*

1.   Time Frame:

                                      Tasks:

                                      Task Responsibility:

2.   Time Frame:

                                      Tasks:

                                      Task Responsibility:

3.   Time Frame:

                                      Tasks:

                                      Task Responsibility:

✎ MAKING THINGS EASIER

Use this form to brainstorm possible A-plus convenience ideas. How might your organization make the customer's experience with you easier (e.g., reduce redundancies, paperwork, or other inconveniences for the customer)? Working alone or with a small group, jot down as many ideas as possible without regard for whether they are practical or immediately usable. Then review all ideas for possible adoption by your organization. Put a checkmark next to the ones you want to try.

☐
☐
☐
☐
☐

Develop a priority list indicating when you will apply each selected idea. Describe tasks or resources necessary to enact the A-plus ideas.

How to Make It Easier on the Customer	*Implementation Requirements*
1.	Time Frame:
	Tasks:
	Task Responsibility:
2.	Time Frame:
	Tasks:
	Task Responsibility:
3.	Time Frame:
	Tasks:
	Task Responsibility:

✍ SIMPLIFYING PRODUCTS

Use this form to brainstorm possible A-plus convenience ideas. How might your organization make your products or services simpler for you customer? Working alone or with a small group, jot down as many ideas as possible without regard for whether they are practical or immediately usable. Then review all ideas for possible adoption by your organization. Put a checkmark next to the ones you want to try.

☐
☐
☐
☐
☐

Develop a priority list indicating when you will apply each selected idea. Describe tasks or resources necessary to enact the A-plus ideas.

Ideas for Simplifying Your Products/Services	*Implementation Requirements*
1.	Time Frame:
	Tasks:
	Task Responsibility:
2.	Time Frame:
	Tasks:
	Task Responsibility:
3.	Time Frame:
	Tasks:
	Task Responsibility:

Notes

1. Douglas A. Blackmon, "The Milkman Returns—with Much More," *The Wall Street Journal* (December 15, 1999), p. B1.
2. Jane Bennett Clarke, "Washed, Cooked and Priced to Go," *Kiplinger's Personal Finance* (January 2000), p. 135.
3. Joseph B. Cahill, "The Secret Weapon of Big Discounters: Lowly Shopping Carts," *The Wall Street Journal* (November 24, 1999), p. 1.
4. Calmetta Y. Coleman, "Making Malls (Gasp!) Convenient," *The Wall Street Journal* (February 8, 2000), p. B1.
5. Joel A. Baglole, "Loblaw's Supermarkets Add Fitness Clubs to Offerings," *The Wall Street Journal* (December 27, 1999), p. B4.
6. Hilary Stout, "The Ad Budget: Zero. The Buzz: Deafening," *The Wall Street Journal European Edition* (December 30, 1999), p. 4.
7. "Worst Customer Service," reported in *Parade Magazine* (December 26, 1999), p. 13.

Chapter 9

Actualizing the A-Plus Customer Loyalty Strategy

Until a concept becomes experience, all there is, is speculation.

—Neale Donald Walsh, *Conversations with God*

The Way It Is . . .

At a conference once I heard a speaker say, "If I was down to my last two dollars, I'd spend one of them on training and the other on marketing." I tend to agree, and apparently so does Sabena Airlines of Belgium. In the airline's in-flight magazine, Sabena describes its Welcome Now project that focuses on the personal touch in customer service.

"Sabena Group's 12,000-employee staff takes part in seminars that reinforce our key objectives: paying attention to your individual needs; offering quick solutions when things go wrong; and inspiring your confidence by providing you at once with accurate information." The article goes on to describe the extensive commitment the company has made to ongoing training of all employees. The seminar content is based on feedback gathered from customers and employees at all levels, "from catering and baggage staff to senior management."[1]

Every day thousands of companies around the world consider ways to improve customer service, strengthen customer relationships, and build customer loyalty. Managers and leaders seek to evaluate how the organization is doing and come up with new ideas for reducing customer turnoffs in value, systems, and people. The better leaders may also search for ways to A-plus their customers. They may not use the terminology used in this book, but they wrestle with achieving the same end result.

Each of these management functions involves people. And getting people to do things is like herding cats. Herein lies the universal challenge of management: accomplishing work with and through other people. If managers try to fly solo, to do it all alone, the likelihood of success drops dramatically. Group involvement at all levels (as promoted in Sabena's project) is essential to actualizing an A-plus strategy.

SELF-EVALUATION: SOME POTENTIALLY DISQUIETING QUESTIONS MANAGERS NEED TO ANSWER

Before we get into the specifics of this chapter, ask yourself a few tough questions about how well your organization is doing with its customer service efforts. Take a few moments to answer yes or no to each of the following questions. Does your company, organization, or department:

1. Talk about customer service but pay frontline people a low, flat wage?   Y   N
2. Offer little or no training in specific skills associated with service for customer-contact people?   Y   N
3. Offer no special incentives for taking care of the customer?   Y   N
4. Punish or reprimand employees' poor customer service, but take good service for granted?   Y   N
5. Place greater emphasis on winning new customers than retaining ones it already has?   Y   N
6. Offer no awards or recognition for non–customer-contact employees' efforts to serve customers?   Y   N
7. Hold "be nice to the customer" programs or campaigns that last for a few weeks or months but are soon forgotten?   Y   N
8. Have top managers who rarely (if ever) devote time to listening to customers and helping them solve problems?   Y   N
9. Make no effort to measure service quality as perceived by customers?   Y   N

10. Make no attempt to hold managers accountable for loyalty building—or to reward them for improved customer loyalty levels?
Y N

Most organizations would have to answer yes to at least several of these questions. That, in itself, is not an indicator of poor service policies, but it could point to some potential problem areas that may be hampering an A-plus strategy implementation. A yes response to a few of these questions may not be devastating, but if the answer is yes to most of them, the organization is likely to face an uphill battle to substantially improve customer loyalty.

Select the two or three questions that you feel reflect the most serious potential barriers to building customer loyalty in your organization. Develop a plan of action to overcome the problem suggested by the question.

The Functions of Management in Building Customer Loyalty

Successfully implementing a customer loyalty strategy calls for creatively applying the four key management functions:

1. Planning
2. Organizing
3. Motivating
4. Controlling

In this chapter we look at each function as it relates to the creation and actualization of an A-plus strategy. This quick review of management tasks is intended as a reminder, certainly not as new information. Stepping back and taking a back-to-basics look at the process in the context of customer loyalty can be helpful.

Planning an A-Plus Strategy

Effective planning includes both big-picture thinking (e.g., setting a vision, developing objectives, and gathering the resources needed) and shorter-term implementation activities. Big-picture planning usually involves intensive strategy development and the articulation of foundation concepts upon which the company's overall efforts are to be based.

The manager's daily planning actions should look ahead to what must be done to maintain and improve performance, solve problems, and develop employee competence. When planning, a manager sets objectives in performance areas and identifies key tasks that are to be pursued this week, this month, and this year. Having set these objectives, the manager then thinks through such questions as:

- → What specific tasks are to be done to reach these objectives?
- → Who will carry out these activities?
- → When will these activities take place?
- → Where will this work be done?
- → What resources will be needed?

Such planning should be based on information received from customers, organization members, and other stakeholders. Throughout this book I have shown you ways to gather perceptions and hard data from and about customers. The planning process involves:

- → Consistently, persistently gathering good-quality information
- → Using the information to implement and adjust an ongoing strategy using the seven strategies discussed in this book

Planning an A-plus strategy calls for both big-picture thinking and ongoing planning based on consistent data gathering.

Articulate a Vision

Management should articulate a vision for customer relationships. But— and this is very important—vision statements should be developed as a group process. Vision or mission statements proclaimed by managers without input from organization members are seen as fiats and have less power to influence individual behavior than do statements developed with the participation of the people responsible for making the vision a reality.

If your company has no customer mission statement and has not articulated a vision in a concise, memorable form, or if the statement has gotten stale, work with your people to articulate a fresh theme or credo—a customer loyalty mission statement.

//
Use group input to develop a concise, memorable mission statement regarding your customers.
//

As I consult with organizations, I typically ask if they have a customer service theme or credo. Fairly often I get answers along the lines of: "Oh, yes, we have thirteen points to excellent customer service." My reply to that is, "Oh, really? What's point eleven?" The manager may say, "Well, I don't know exactly." Then I ask, "Well, how about point six? Which one's that?" And again the typical answer is, "I'm not sure. I actually haven't memorized all these things, but we have these points posted in every store."

Unfortunately, that doesn't do much good. To articulate a theme means to come up with a succinct, clear statement of what the organization is about and how it can be seen as unique in the eyes of the customer. Someone once said that a good mission statement is one that "you could repeat at gunpoint!" Such a statement provides essential information that every employee can remember and buy into as a guiding statement that shapes their actions and helps them make decisions.

//
A good mission statement could be repeated at gunpoint!
//

Let's look at a few examples of well-expressed mission statements. Federal Express says it in three words: "Absolutely, positively, overnight." The company will get the packages there absolutely, positively, overnight, and FedEx is 99.8 percent successful at doing that. Direct marketing clothier Lands' End has a simple motto/credo that has just two words: "Guaranteed. Period." Both of these themes communicate the company's highest customer service priority.

A *Harvard Business Review*[2] article told of a Seattle restaurant staff that wrestled with this idea of creating a simple, clear theme for the business. After carefully looking at the company through the eyes of their customer—"just what do our restaurant guests want from us?"—the staff came up with this theme: "Your enjoyment guaranteed. Always." That is exactly what they offer their guests, enjoyment.

The employees made the theme into an acronym: YEGA. While YEGA may not mean anything to most of us, it became a catchword for the organization. They developed YEGA promotions and YEGA bucks and YEGA pins and hats to get employees involved in the spirit of YEGA. It was fun, it was interesting, and it reminded the employees constantly of that simple four-word theme: "Your enjoyment guaranteed. Always."

To fulfill the management responsibility of articulating a good theme for your business, you must:

→ Commit to work on the process of identifying a theme that is succinct, clear, and descriptive of your uniqueness.

→ Gather ideas from customers. Ask them, "What five things do you, as a customer, want in doing business with us?" Ask them to respond quickly, off the top of their head, and then look closely at the language they use. They may respond with terms such as "low process," "friendly," "fun," and "wide assortment of goods." Look for terms that come up repeatedly. Also, pay special attention to the first few terms expressed. These are usually the most salient feelings.

→ Gather ideas from employees. Get employees together in the organization and ask, "If you were our customer, what five things would you like to get from a company like ours?" Again, ask people to respond quickly. Jot down the language and then collect all of the words.

As you gather perceptions from customers and employees, you'll likely notice that some terms come up over and over again. These typically are the kinds of words that reassure your customer. These are good words to put into your customer service theme.

Look carefully at the language your customers use when articulating your theme.

In drafting a theme remember that:

→ *Participation of and input from both customers and employees are vital.* The customers can best tell you what they're looking for in an organization like yours, and the employees' participation will ensure that they accept and hopefully live by the intention of the theme. Studies have shown time and again that by having employees participate in clarifying a theme, they will feel more committed to it. Frontline people know the customers best and can give great ideas on how to better serve them. Never overlook the ideas of this group of experts. The employees on the firing line have the best ideas. Use them.

→ *Writing several rough drafts of the theme is necessary; don't be too quick to come up with the finished version.* Phrase the final version in ten words or fewer.

→ *Writing the theme as an acronym can make it easier to remember.* The YEGA example given earlier is one such acronym. (This is not mandatory, of course, but can be useful.)

When you've identified a statement of uniqueness, ask yourself the question, Would everyone in the organization choose roughly the same words you chose to describe our distinctiveness?

Once articulated, be sure the theme is communicated often. Make it a regular part of any company communication effort. Print it on company letterhead; repeat it regularly at company meetings; tell your customers what it is. In short, be redundant and reinforce it to anyone who will listen.

Communicate your theme or vision statement often; repetition is important.

A simple way to verify whether your people are buying in to the vision is to grab some of your employees and ask them to describe the organization's theme. Especially invite an employee who's been with the organization for ten days or less to identify the theme. If he or she can't do it, make the theme a more prominent part of new employee orientation.

What good does it do just to be able to repeat such a phrase? The answer is that it's a start. Repeating some words may seem meaningless at first, but eventually the sense of the statement will sink in and people will adjust their behaviors to act congruently with the vision. Most organizations fall far short of even that level of agreement. Focusing people on a common theme can be well worth the effort.

One final note: A theme is not necessarily forever. As an organization changes direction, as markets or economic conditions change, a theme may be modified. Some organizations may want to use a theme statement for a limited period of time much the way advertisers use an ad slogan for only a few years. Modifying the theme should not, however, be done without careful thought. Consistency of direction is in itself valuable.

Consider the Use of Consultants

At the risk of sounding self-serving, consider retaining a qualified consultant as you plan and implement a customer loyalty strategy. A qualified consultant can take a detached, global view. He or she can peruse the forest without getting too tangled in the trees. Ideas and applications used with other client organizations can be brought to the table and the strategy launch can happen without taking managers away from other duties.

With my clients, I present a process that outlines their responsibilities and mine. The guidelines are clear and the process moves forward systematically when a conscientious consultant brings expertise to the table. (A sample of a generic consulting proposal I use and that you can use as well is shown in Appendix A.)

Organizing and Staffing for Loyalty Building

The management task of organizing involves arranging the work sequence and assigning areas of responsibility and authority. Having determined the benchmarks, set initials goals, and determined activities of the various work units, the manager's next task is to:

→ Assign responsibilities to specific employees or workgroups.

→ Give employees the supporting authority to fulfill their responsibilities (i.e., empowerment).

Organize People and Delineate Authority

The organizing function involves such actions as clarifying the organizational structure (e.g., who reports to whom, what functions or departments coordinate with each other), assigning certain responsibilities, and giving authority to organization members. People at all levels need to know the scope and range of their jobs. Employees need to understand what they can or cannot do for the customer.

Among companies giving legendary service, people at all levels are given a lot of latitude. Nordstrom employees know they can do almost anything to meet a customer's needs. They have been known to send clothing to customers using overnight delivery (regardless of the additional cost) and to give customers gifts or additional merchandise to recompense for any customer disappointment. Ritz-Carlton Hotel employees are encouraged to take personal ownership of any problem a guest may have. If a guest's need comes to their attention, they are fully empowered to drop what they are doing and solve the problem or meet the guest's need. Bellhops have been known to rush out of the hotel to buy a magazine for a guest who was disappointed that the publication wasn't available in the hotel's gift shop. No questions asked, managers have given employees at all levels the authority to do whatever it takes.

By contrast, an auto dealership committed to a no-dicker, fixed-price policy carries it too far in prohibiting its employees from providing anything extra for customers. At one such dealership, a salesperson can literally be fired for giving customers a free set of floor mats, for example. Even if sales representatives buy these out of their own money, they would be reprimanded and perhaps fired for doing so. This is not the way to go. It defeats everything that an A-plus strategy stands for and, I believe, virtually destroys all opportunity for building customer loyalty.

///
Delineating authority today means empowering employees at all levels.
///

Saddling workers with unnecessary restrictions kills off many loyalty-building opportunities.

Staff with Quality Employees

Managers are responsible for recruiting qualified people for each employee position, orienting new people to the company's service expectations, and providing training so that people become proficient by instruction and practice.

Some successful managers recruit by stealing good employees from other companies. (That's stated a bit strong, but the principle works.) As managers encounter people with great attitudes and excellent customer service skills, they may try to hire them away or at least recommend them to company recruiters.

One owner of a chain of fast-food restaurants solved the problem of getting quality people in a high-turnover industry by giving his business card to employees of other companies who wait on him. He'd say something like, "Thank you for your great service. You did a nice job. If you are ever interested in changing jobs, I'd appreciate it if you'd call me personally. I'm sure I could find a place for you in my organization."

Keep a file of people you'd like to have working for you and, when an opening occurs, contact them. Don't worry if they are working in a totally different type of business. The specifics of your organization can be taught. Great attitudes cannot.

Hire People with Emotional Intelligence

A key characteristic of effective customer-contact people is emotional intelligence (EI). EI refers to an assortment of noncognitive skills, capabilities, and competencies that influence a person's ability to succeed in coping with environmental demands and pressures—especially other people. People with high EI have developed these attributes:

* Self-awareness, or the ability to know what they are feeling
* Self-management, or the ability to manage their own emotions and impulses
* Self-motivation, or the ability to persist in the face of setbacks and failures

+ Empathy, or the ability to sense how others are feeling
+ Social skills, or the ability to handle the emotions of others

The research into emotional intelligence suggests that employers should consider it in selection, especially in jobs that demand a high degree of social interaction.[3]

Be Sure Your People Have Everything They Need

Once you have recruited good people, be certain that they have everything they need to do a great job. Be sure that everyone who needs them can find the following resources:

+ A telephone in a place where it can be heard
+ A computer with customer records
+ A fax machine, messenger service, or supplies for overnight shipping
+ Letterhead, envelopes, and postage
+ Business cards (maybe even the new electronic "cards" that are played in a CD-ROM drive)
+ Product information, pricing schedules, and publications
+ Policy statements and a printed copy of the company's vision statement
+ A desk, writing table, or private place to confer with customers
+ Office supplies
+ A mobile or portable phone

These requirements will differ among various organizations, but today's customer loyalty efforts demand today's equipment.

Create Growth Opportunities for Employees

Managers also need to be sure that people, once hired, have ample opportunity to develop their knowledge, attitudes, and skills. The best jobs are those that allow people to grow.

Provide employees with ample training and frequent opportunities to develop their skills. Use the many media available to provide training, including classes, seminars, videotape programs, and online courses.

Leading and Motivating

Managers lead by enabling the organization to achieve its objectives. To do this, managers must:

+ Show the direction in which subordinates must go and model the behaviors.

    + Generate the energy (i.e., motivation) that subordinates must feel.

    + Provide the resources people need to accomplish tasks.

An organization's leaders set the tone for motivation throughout the workplace. Motivation can be simply defined as providing motives for action. Leaders provide motives or reasons why people should act in particular ways. They also motivate by persuading and inspiring people to take desired action. And, of course, the best leaders motivate by example, not by edict.

//

Motivation is an ongoing management responsibility. We motivate best by modeling the behaviors we want from our employees.

//

Direct the Company's Efforts

Managers fulfill their leadership functions by directing and delegating. This means assigning responsibility and accountability for service results to the people they manage. Other directing functions include coordinating desired efforts in the most efficient combinations, managing differences, resolving conflicts, and stimulating creativity and innovation in achieving service goals.

Gaining employee participation can make directing go much easier. People who willingly volunteer to be responsible for some functions are more likely to be committed to these jobs than people who are just assigned a task. Invite people to take charge of portions of your loyalty-building efforts. For example, rotate the responsibility for gathering and reporting on service measures. Let different people see, firsthand, the kinds of feedback you are getting and invite them to take charge of efforts to remedy certain problems.

Adjust or Modify the Reward System

Many companies fall into the trap of rewarding one kind of behavior while hoping employees will produce other ones. A commonplace example is the process of paying people by the hour. What behavior is this encouraging? Taking up hours! Is that what you want your people to do?

A clothing store set up an incentive program whereby the top salesperson won a substantial cash award, yet the same store encouraged employees to work together to meet customer needs. Did it get employee cooperation? No. It got salespeople climbing all over each other to get to the customer before another salesperson did.

Think about the behaviors you really want to see practiced in your organization. Then reward those behaviors, not something else. Also, think carefully about whether you want to provide group or individual rewards. Much of customer service is a team effort, so you may want to consider creative use of group rewards.

One client I worked with for several years created what it called the Excel program. Employees throughout the organization were awarded Excel points for such things as:

+ Receiving an unsolicited compliment from a customer
+ Being recognized by their department manager for exceptional service effort or problem handling
+ Being "caught" doing something exceptional by other organization managers
+ Reading the company service newsletter and completing a brief quiz in the publication
+ Attending optional training sessions or classes

Each of these actions earned a certain number of points. At the end of each month, the employee from each department with the most points was selected to attend the "Excel-ebration" where a luncheon was served and participants played games for prizes. The prizes were modest (e.g., dinner certificates, movie passes, small appliances, or tools) but the comradeship was strong and people felt good about the attention they received.

At the end of the year, the company held a bigger Excel-ebration. The top point winners from each department for the year were invited, along with a spouse or companion, to a beautiful dinner. There were more contests as well, though this time the prizes were more substantial: TVs, exercise equipment, stereos, mountain bikes, and vacation packages.

The Excel program generated great interest and helped sustain ongoing motivation among employees to treat customers right.

///

Ongoing motivation can be built with special incentive programs. Be certain that the behaviors used to qualify for the incentives are consistent with loyalty building.

///

Controlling and Evaluating Results

The last basic management function involves comparing actual results to expected or planned-for results so as to identify any deviation from plan. Typically, any deviation from plan calls for adjusting motivation attempts, replanning of activities in order to close the gap, or changing the objectives to be more realistic.

Customer loyalty is a critical organizational goal and should be one of the most closely watched indicators of success. This book has suggested a number of ways to assess how you are doing, some more formal than others. Benchmarking is critical to measure changes. But some simple, informal assessments can also provide a good feel for how the company is doing. One simple method is to simply ask many questions.

Manage with Questions

Author Bill Maynard[4] agrees that the art of management often involves asking lots of questions. He recommends that as managers interact with people throughout the organization as well as with customers, they ask questions such as these:

What made you mad today?
What took too long?
What caused complaints today?
What was misunderstood today?
What costs too much?

What was too complicated?
What was just plain silly?
What job involved too many people?
What job involved too many actions?
What was wasted?

Commit these questions to memory and ask them often. Then, of course, it is crucial that managers act to the degree possible on the answers people give.

///
Part of the controlling process should be to simply ask many questions about how the company could better build customer loyalty.
///

Harvesting A-Plus Ideas

The single most effective thing a company can do to launch and sustain an A-plus strategy is systematically harvest ideas. Every employee should have available a forum where he or she can offer A-plus ideas or participate in deciding what ideas to implement. The final management task needed to actualize an A-plus strategy is, therefore, gathering an ongoing flow of A-plus ideas that can make your organization consistently stronger in attracting and keeping customers.

Set aside some specific time for A-plus idea generation. Early in the strategy-implementation process you may want to use an off-site retreat or specially designated launch meeting. But once your A-plus strategy is up and running, you should consistently designate additional times to gather ideas. Many of my clients use a few minutes as part of regularly scheduled meetings dedicated to one strategy (e.g., A-plus convenience or A-plus value ideas) or even a subportion of a strategy (e.g., speed of service or add-ons). That may be all the time that's needed to ensure a constant flow of ideas.

///
Ongoing attention to idea generation is crucial to a successful A-plus strategy. Be certain all employees have regular opportunities to contribute.
///

Please remember that people at all organizational levels can and will provide great A-plus ideas. I worked with a hospital client that did a great job of getting its employees involved. As a part of regular staff meetings, department supervisors designated some time to brainstorm possible A-plus ideas. To make the process more manageable, they would focus on one opportunity area at a time.

The housekeeping department (janitors and maids) at this hospital came up with an interesting A-plus idea that illustrates the potential of this strategy. Although at the low end of the organizational food chain, these people were fully empowered to participate. One meeting produced the idea to change the paintings on the walls of the hospital corridors periodically so that patients, especially long-term patients, would have something different to look at. A little thing, but to the elderly patients, who could come out of a room for perhaps only a few minutes each day, it was a thoughtful gesture.

The payoff came one day when a janitor was mopping the hallway and an older woman came out of her room and was admiring a painting. She commented on how lovely the painting was, and the housekeeping employee put down his mop, came over to her, and said, "Ma'am, we change the pictures every week so that you'll have something different to look at." The patient was deeply touched by this gesture of kindness.

This story illustrates several themes discussed throughout this book:

+ Little things can have considerable impact on customers.
+ Employees at all levels of an organization have good ideas.
+ Given the opportunity to input their ideas, people can and will have a dramatic effect on customer perceptions of the organization.

Use Brainstorming When Creative Ideas Are Needed

The term *brainstorming* has become synonymous with any kind of creative thinking. But that misuses the word. Brainstorming is a specific technique using explicit rules for idea generation and development. This approach requires a communication climate in which the free expression of all kinds of ideas is valued and encouraged, no matter how offbeat or bizarre they may seem. There are four basic rules for a brainstorming session:

1. Do not criticize any ideas. Permit no comments, no grunts or groans, no thumbs-down gestures. Just let all ideas come out and record them.

2. Never disqualify an idea as being too wild.

3. Generate the maximum quantity (don't worry about quality yet). Push to get as many ideas without regard to whether they make any sense at this point.

4. Seize opportunities to hitchhike (i.e., add to or amplify) ideas suggested by others.

The rules of brainstorming are easier to state than to obey—especially the second one. Unless great care is taken, nonverbal cues can be interpreted as judgments of ideas, which can discourage additional "wild ideas." Avoid that. During a brainstorming session, these rules should be prominently posted as a constant reminder to all participants.

The climate that's set by the meeting leader can promote or hamper the use of brainstorming. A climate that encourages humor and informality works best. So go into a rubber room and have some fun. The nuttiest ideas can sometimes be refined into something workable and ingenious.

Use a Nominal Group Process When Appropriate

Another approach useful in harvesting ideas is the nominal group process (NGP). This is an idea-generating approach that is particularly useful when dealing with potentially emotional, unusually creative, or controversial ideas. The process works as follows:

1. *Silent Generation of Solution Ideas in Writing.* Rather than having group members immediately speak up with their point of view (a process that may commit them to that view since they've voiced it "publicly"), the NGP has participants write down ideas, privately. Following a clear definition of the problem or issues, group members spend ten to twenty minutes writing out their ideas about possible solutions.

2. *Round-Robin Recording of Ideas.* Each participant provides one idea from his or her list, which is written on a flip chart in full view of the group. Ideas are recorded but not discussed at this point. This round-

robin listing of ideas continues until the participants have no further ideas.

3. *Discussion of Ideas for Clarification.* Once all ideas are recorded, people may then clarify or amplify up on an idea.

4. *Voting by Ranking Items.* Then a silent vote is taken where participants rank-order the ideas. Several votes may be needed before a final solution is accepted.

Use brainstorming and NGP to gather ideas from all organization members. Make the harvesting process ongoing. In doing so, you consistently raise the bar and further distinguish your company's unique approach to customer loyalty.

Make idea-harvesting an ongoing and systematic process using techniques such as brainstorming and the nominal group process.

A Quick Summary: Seven Tasks to Initiate and Sustain the A-Plus Customer Loyalty Strategy

Managers can turn good intentions into a workable A-plus strategy by implementing the seven key tasks briefly described here. These need not always be done in the order presented; several may be done concurrently.

Task 1: Orient All Employees

Take steps to ensure that all employees clearly understand the need for cultivating customer loyalty. Teach them about the cost of lost customers, how lost customers lead to lost jobs, why poor service givers pay a psychological price, and why it is in their best interest to develop customer service professionalism. This step can best be done via a series of training sessions (and by providing all organization members with copies of this book). Orienting employees in this way gets them all speaking the same language and singing from the same sheet music.

Task 2: Build Momentum

Conduct regular follow-up departmental meetings after the initial training. Teach basic creativity and group problem-solving skills, then schedule and conduct regular brainstorming sessions to discuss possible new A-plus ideas. Show individuals and work groups how to set departmental or team goals.

Construct or modify the reward system so that the most useful activities get the best rewards. Create a reward committee to determine a budget, identify special bonuses, and define criteria whereby people can win the rewards. Then develop data-gathering forms/processes that give credit for good work. Distribute "Attaboy, Attagirl" cards or small rewards to recognize success immediately.

Task 3: Monitor Customer Expectation and Employee Behavior

Teach naive listening techniques (discussed in Chapter 4) to employees and managing-by-questions approaches to supervisors. Recognize the value of unhappy customers as sources of improvement ideas. Schedule focus groups regularly, on a calendar. Record, digest, and keep data and trends analysis.

At the same time, conduct regular shopper surveys to determine the type of service that people are getting from employees. These surveys should typically be done by independent "mystery shopper" services that can provide immediate and specific feedback to employees. Mystery shoppers are researchers who pose as customers for the purpose of gathering observational data. They typically use a checksheet to record employee behaviors and company conditions.

Task 4: Establish Systematic Customer Retention/Follow-Up Efforts

Develop creative customer follow-up techniques. Schedule regular follow-up with mailouts, phone calls, announcements, and special incentives. Try other loyalty builders such as customer photos or customer letters posted on display. Perhaps acknowledge a "Customer of the Month" or make a similar recognition.

Task 5: Provide Continuous Training for Employees

Schedule repeat "basic" training for new employees. Also schedule regular continuation training whereby employees can receive instruction on tasks such as writing customer correspondence, handling difficult people, improving telephone techniques, and mastering time and task management.

Task 6: Conduct Ongoing Systems Reviews

Create a task force to review systems. Employ explorer groups to visit competitors or similar businesses that have good ideas you can learn to apply. Create a suggestion program, too. The focus of this program is to improve systems by announcing and publicizing suggestions, budgeting award money, creating forms for submitting ideas, and forming a review committee to evaluate suggestions submitted.

Task 7: Recruit, Develop, and Retain Excellent Employees

Attract and select exceptional service personnel by developing aptitude/attitude testing and interviewing procedures. Proactively invite promising employees from other businesses to join your organization.

Once employees are hired, be sure they understand the organization's promotional criteria and that you clearly tie these criteria to the customer service reward system. In short, base employee advancement on service attitudes and skills. As part of this process, be sure to conduct meaningful performance reviews with service criteria being measured and factored into review.

A Final Thought

The ideas in this book will do you no good until you put them into practice. Companies can talk about customer loyalty until they are blue in the face, but until they apply the tactics and strategies described in this book, nothing much is likely to happen. If they keep doing what they've always done, they'll keep getting what they've always gotten.

I hope you are motivated to try on some of the behaviors described in these nine chapters. I have intentionally kept the book concise in the hope that you will read and reread these ideas many times and, more important, that you will implement them.

Try on the seven power strategies and see what happens. With them you have at your disposal a proven process for translating good intentions into a realistic, workable strategy for building unprecedented levels of customer loyalty.

As the famous footwear ads so succinctly put it: *Just do it.*

WORKSHEETS:
ACTUALIZING A CUSTOMER LOYALTY STRATEGY

✍ PLANNING IDEA

Review the ideas in this chapter about planning and implementing an A-plus strategy. What specific management tasks should you focus on now? Jot down any ideas that come to mind. Ideas you might start with are benchmarking, articulating and communicating a theme, setting goals, or employing a consultant or outside adviser. What are your organization's top priorities?

☐

☐

☐

☐

☐

Review your list and place a checkmark next to the top two or three actions you should give priority attention to. Then develop a plan for implementing each idea.

ORGANIZING AND STAFFING IDEAS

Review the ideas in this chapter about organizing and staffing an A-plus strategy. Examples include assigning job responsibilities, giving employees additional authority, hiring quality employees, and finding out more about emotional intelligence. What specific management tasks should you focus on now? Jot down any new ideas that come to mind. What are your organization's top priorities?

☐
☐
☐
☐
☐

Review your list and place a checkmark next to the top two or three actions you should give priority attention to. Then develop a plan for implementing each.

◤ LEADING AND MOTIVATING IDEAS

Review the ideas in this chapter about leading and motivating an A-plus strategy. Examples include assigning accountability for certain results areas, adjusting the reward system, initiating special incentive programs, and leading by example. What specific management tasks should you focus on now? Jot down any new ideas that come to mind. What are your organization's top priorities?

☐
☐
☐
☐
☐

Review your list and place a checkmark next to the top two or three actions you should give priority attention to. Then develop a plan for implementing each.

CONTROL AND MEASUREMENT IDEAS

Review the ideas in this chapter about controlling, evaluating, and measuring a strategy. Examples include managing by questions and involving employees in measurement and analysis. What specific management tasks should you focus on now? Jot down any new ideas that come to mind. What are your organization's top priorities?

☐
☐
☐
☐
☐

Review your list and place a checkmark next to the top two or three actions you should give priority attention to. Then develop a plan for implementing each.

Notes

1. "Small Details Can Make a World of Difference," Sabena *Passport* (December 1999–January 2000), p. 9.
2. T. W. Firnstahl, "My Employees Are My Service Guarantee," *Harvard Business Review* (July–August 1989), pp. 28–32.
3. This description of emotional intelligence is adapted from Steven P. Robbins, *Essentials of Organizational Behavior*, 6th ed. (Upper Saddle River, N.J.: Prentice-Hall, 2000), pp. 40–41. The concept of EI was first developed by Daniel Goleman in his book *Working with Emotional Intelligence* (New York: Bantam, 1998).
4. Bill Maynard, "How to Manage with Questions," in *TeleProfessional*. This newsletter can be purchased by writing to the publisher at 209 W. 5th Street, Waterloo, Iowa 50701-5420.

Appendix A

Sample Generic Consulting Proposal

The following is a sample consulting proposal for implementing the A-plus strategy in an organization. If your organization seeks outside expertise or attempts to launch a strategy using internal staff, this proposal describes an approach that has been used in other organizations. If you are involved with recommending a course of action to your company, this proposal offers a suggested format.

Creating a Customer Loyalty Strategy That Works
Paul R. Timm, Ph.D., Consultant

Loyal customers impact an organization's bottom line more than any advertising campaign or PR effort. Turned-off customers produce devastating ripple effects. The cost of the lost customer quickly dissipates any benefits gained from community relations, advertising, or marketing taken alone. It costs five times as much to generate a new customer than to keep an existing one.

Job number-one must be to build customer loyalty. Companies do this by exceeding, in positive ways, what customers anticipate from their core products or service and from the whole experience of doing business with the organization.

This approach to creating a strategy virtually guarantees enhanced customer satisfaction, loyalty, and retention. This approach does not rely on chance or luck. It provides the tools and direction needed for all members of the organization to play important roles in creating and maintaining customer satisfaction. It empowers people. It builds a firm foundation for long-term growth and constant quality improvement.

Long-term, incremental improvements add a dynamic quality to the strategy and breathe life into the process.

Perhaps the most serious mistake leaders make in implementing loyalty-building efforts is to convey to employees that these constitute a new program or campaign. From the very beginning, it is crucial to stress that a customer satisfaction strategy is not a one-time program but rather an ongoing philosophy—a way the company will be doing business over the long term.

Maintaining Enthusiasm Requires Continued Focus

The challenges facing the organization as it initiates a customer satisfaction strategy are to:

1. Convince employees that management is serious about consistent improvement in customer service. Management's emphasis is not a passing fad or empty slogan. The organization will provide resources to make the strategy work.

2. Provide the tools that employees need in the form of additional training and motivation to apply and use the techniques of customer satisfaction excellence.

3. Create or modify reward systems to support the strategy.

4. Create consistency of emphasis on the strategy so that there can be no illusions that "this too shall pass."

5. Supply employees with the expertise they need to solve customer satisfaction problems.

6. Publicize the customer satisfaction efforts so that various stakeholders (e.g., customers, potential customers, employees, the community, shareholders) are aware of the results.

7. Empower and involve all company personnel in the evolution and growth of the strategy.

The Implementation Approach

This typical approach for implementing a successful customer satisfaction strategy is based on proven procedures and reflects a theoretically sound and highly practical way of translating current thinking on customer satisfaction into a systematic plan of action.

Critical Elements Needed for Any Approach to Work

Any approach to enhancing customer satisfaction must meet these criteria:

1. *Top Management Support.* The degree of enthusiasm demonstrated by management will reflect throughout the organization. Managers must buy into the effort and communicate their support to employees at all levels.

2. *Training and Motivation.* Dynamic, interesting training sessions help employees see "what's in it for them" and create the excitement and commitment needed for ongoing success.

3. *Employee Involvement and Empowerment.* Staff at all levels of the company need to be encouraged to participate by offering suggestions, attending brainstorming sessions, and acknowledging service excellence.

The strategy developed with your company should be uniquely applicable to your organization's people and culture. Typically such development involves three major phases:

1. Strategic planning and needs assessment
2. Training and motivation (managers first, then staff)
3. Continuation support (including follow-up training)

Three Phases of a Typical Strategy Development

The following table outlines the requirements of both the consulting team and the client organization. (Note: These activities are not in chronological order. Some activities overlap.)

Consultant Responsibility	Client Responsibility

Strategic Planning and Needs Assessment Phase

☐ Conduct needs assessment	☐ Participate and offer support
☐ Conduct pre-testing	☐ Assign manager most involved
☐ Determine objectives	with implementation (the
☐ Analyze customer data and/or	program "champion")
focus groups	☐ Arrange access to data or set
	up focus group participants

Training and Motivation Phase

☐ Arrange manager's retreat and	☐ Schedule managers' training
strategy launch	(off-site location)
☐ Arrange training "super-sessions" for all employees	☐ Arrange for all employees (including managers) to attend
that include:	super-sessions
↦ Importance of customer loyalty	
↦ Attitudes toward serving	
↦ Communication skills	
↦ "A-plus" customer loyalty	
↦ Buy-in activities	

Continuation Support (Follow-up)

☐ Conduct post-testing	☐ Participate
☐ Complete mailouts to line	☐ Publicize and encourage
managers on a regular basis	attendance
☐ Design nonmandatory training	☐ Create A-plus rewards system
sessions on related topics for	and celebrations
reinforcement	
☐ Assist in developing reward	
program	
☐ Create regular repeats on	
super-session for new hires	
☐ Create materials for company	
newsletter and/or press	
releases	

Appendix B

A Quick Review of the Seven Power Strategies

Strategy 1: Identify Customer Turnoffs

➤ No organization can totally avoid turning off customers at times. The average American company will lose 10 percent to 30 percent of its customers this year—mostly because of poor service. When customers have a choice, they'll go to the competition almost one-third of the time.

➤ Customer satisfaction is like an election held every day, and the people vote with their feet. If dissatisfied, they walk (sometimes run) to your competitor. When your customers don't have a choice—such as in dealing with public utilities or government agencies—they'll use their feet for something else: They'll kick you.

➤ Customer dissatisfaction can erupt in the form of animosity directed toward you and your organization. The psychological toll on employees can result in higher turnover and additional costs, as these burned-out workers need to be retrained or replaced.

➤ Organizations that use an effective customer loyalty strategy have seen profits jump 25 percent to 100 percent. Nonprofit groups see reduced turnover, better financial results—and happier staffs.

➤ Like it or not, customer loyalty is the competitive battleground for the twenty-first century. In fact, it will always be the decisive battleground.

➤ Customer turnoffs can be classified into three categories: value, systems, and people:

➔ Value turnoffs need to be addressed by executive management because they decide the quality level of products and services to be offered.

➔ Systems turnoffs (which include any policies, processes, or procedures that get the company's goods and services to its customers) need to be addressed by management. These almost always require the expenditure of money or other resources to fix.

➔ People turnoffs (mostly communication problems) need to be addressed by all organizational members. Regular communication training can help.

➔ Even when leaders truly believe in the importance of customer service, they still face the difficulty of getting the customer-contact people (often the lowest paid and least well-trained employees) to do what customers want. Examples: A multibillion-dollar fast-food giant places its success squarely in the hands of the minimum-wage teenager taking the orders and delivering the food. The image of a multibillion-dollar bank is created in the mind of the customer by the entry-level teller who handles day-to-day transactions. A multibillion-dollar government agency is judged largely by the receptionist who answers the phone or greets the customer, thus setting the tone for any transaction.

➔ Recognizing turnoffs requires being alert to potential problems and open to customer complaints.

Strategy 2: Recover Dissatisfied Customers

➔ Assuming that an occasional upset customer is of no major consequence to you is a formula for disaster.

➔ The cost of replacing lost customers can be staggering because ripple effects spread the word about dissatisfaction.

➔ Complaining customers can be your best friends. They offer insights that can make your company better—provided you make it easy for them to let you know what they think.

➔ A dissatisfied customer whose complaint is heard and acted upon is more likely to be loyal to your company than a customer who never has a problem.

➔ Expending effort to understand and recover unhappy customers can be one of the best things companies can do. It costs far less to keep a current customer than it does to attract a new one.

➔ Every customer is potentially valuable to your organization and to your career success as a manager.

➔ Only the occasional chronic complainer should be considered dispensable. But even chronic complainers should be subject to your recovery efforts before you give up and send them to your competitors.

Strategy 3: Create Positive Imbalance with Customers

➔ Successful companies earn customer loyalty by constantly seeking ways to meet or exceed what customers anticipate and by strengthening the ongoing relationship with that customer.

➔ You can achieve exceptional customer loyalty levels by creating a psychological imbalance such that your customers believe that they are getting more from you than they "deserve."

➔ Exceeding what customers anticipate from you will create the positive imbalance that is likely to motivate customers to be repeat buyers.

➔ To apply the principle of positive imbalance, you need to constantly sharpen your perception of what customers anticipate and then exceed the customer's expectation in some small but positive and meaningful ways.

➔ Little things can make all the difference. You need not be dramatically different from your competition to earn customer loyalty. Little surprises can reap customer loyalty.

➔ Companies can exceed customer anticipations (i.e., create A-plus conditions) by offering an enhanced sense of value, a more pleasant personality, better information, or additional convenience.

Strategy 4: Give Customers A-Plus Value

➔ Perceived value is a function of price and product quality.

➔ Companies can create A-plus value by giving more than the customer anticipates.

→ A-plus value is both tangible and perceptual. The goal is to create an enhanced *sense* of value that exceeds what the customer anticipated.

→ A-plus value can be created by improving packaging.

→ A-plus value can be created with more attractive guarantees or warranties.

→ A-plus value can arise from better goodness of fit so that customers get the best possible product to meet their individual needs.

→ A-plus value can be achieved when customers have memorable experiences associated with your company.

→ A-plus value can come from customers sharing your company's values, experiencing your uniqueness, or appreciating your high levels of credibility.

→ Build organizational credibility by keeping promises, being straightforward and clear with customers, and avoiding programs, products, or incentives that fail to live up to customer expectations.

Strategy 5: Give Customers A-Plus Information

→ Virtually every product or service has an informational component that customers need or could benefit from.

→ Companies that exceed what customers anticipate with information are more likely to build loyalty.

→ A-plus service can come from a company's willingness to "hold hands" with its customers—to provide assistance or instruction necessary for customers to get the most value from their purchases.

→ A-plus information can be enhanced by careful media choices and creativity in the application of various message delivery channels.

→ A-plus information arises from a company's willingness to constantly strive for better message clarity. This can often be achieved by using graphics, icons, and layout to supplement the words in a message.

→ User groups, classes, and similar events that promote customer participation are additional means to provide A-plus information.

→ A-plus information is especially important in electronic commerce, where too many businesses are making it too difficult for customers to communicate with them. The winners in e-tailing will be those companies that provide A-plus information.

Strategy 6: Show Customers A-Plus Personality

➔ The way employees communicate with customers (verbally and nonverbally) projects personality.

➔ The composite of all employee communication and company culture projects organizational personality.

➔ A-plus personality is projected when friendliness, consideration, and helpfulness exceed what customers anticipate.

➔ A-plus personality stems from treating customers like guests; greeting them, making them feel at home, and getting them involved in some activity if possible.

➔ A-plus personality grows as a company's employees develop rapport with their customers through such acts as smiling, complimenting, calling customers by name, following up on commitments, and some touching behaviors.

➔ A-plus personality arises when companies create and maintain a communication circle with customers by listening, asking for feedback, reassuring the customer's buying decisions, and thanking customers for their business or their feedback.

➔ A-plus personality can be established with excellent telephone skills (something that is lacking in many companies).

➔ The organization's A-plus personality is reflected by its culture. Culture refers to the friendliness of the organization's systems, the appearance and grooming of its members and work areas, its ability to engage in hoopla and fun, and the organizational commitment to ongoing improvement and customer follow-up after the sale.

➔ Companies reinforce A-plus personality behaviors by developing and rewarding its employees in appropriate ways.

Strategy 7: Give Customers A-Plus Convenience

➔ The popularity of home-delivered pizza and auto quick-lube centers typifies the opportunity in nurturing A-plus convenience.

✦ Excellent convenience and speed of service are powerful ways to exceed what customers anticipate from your company. Too many organizations are overly casual about wasting customers' time.

✦ A-plus convenience is created when you set a schedule or deadline that you beat. Example: A delivery promised by 10 A.M. arrives at 9:30.

✦ A-plus convenience means constantly looking for ways to make it easier for customers to do business with you.

✦ A-plus convenience can be achieved by offering ancillary services or convenient tie-ins with other companies.

A-plus convenience arises from simplifying products and reducing cumbersome paperwork.

✦ Managers are wise to constantly monitor customer behaviors to see what is difficult or inconvenient for them. Then, reduce or eliminate the hassle and create A-plus convenience.

Index